You're Not the Boss of Me

Slaying the Inner Critic

Jennifer Adrienne Matwawana

DEDICATION

This book is dedicated to every person who has had to go face to face with their inner critic.

Always remember: your authenticity, who you truly are, is unique.

It's your gift to the world.

Love who you are. Be proud of who you are. Honor who you are.

ACKNOWLEDGMENTS

I am finally finished the editing stage of this book and I'm sitting here reflecting. I am feeling healed, whole, aligned, and brave, very much because of the people who held me when I couldn't hold myself.

To my children and bonus children: Daven, Kobey, Isaiah, Deves, and Julien, and to your partners, wives, and beautiful children, my life has come full circle because of you. I adore you with every part of my heart. Watching you grow, build families, love boldly, and walk your own paths is one of the greatest joys of my life.

To my E.L.I.T.E. sister friends, life with y'all is amazing. You are my laughter, my accountability, my truth-tellers, my soft landing, and my hype team. Thank you for being the kind of women who make womanhood sweeter, safer, and stronger.

To my incredible business partners, Melissa and Shirley, thank you for walking beside me in purpose, in leadership, and in impact. Our work matters, and doing it with you has been one of my greatest professional blessings.

To my parents, my sister, and her family, your love, grounding, and presence have shaped who I am. Thank you for reminding me where I come from and who I was always meant to be.

To my husband, Edo. My love, my calm, my friend. Thank you for your patience, your tenderness, your humor, your consistency, and your steady love. You are one of the best decisions I have ever made, and every day with you is evidence that I chose well.

To God (you know I can't write a book like this and not thank my spiritual daddy!), WOW are you faithful. Thank you. Thank you for the gifts, for the bruises, and for always catching me and carrying me when I fall. THANK YOU.

Finally, to every reader who picks up this book, thank you. Thank you for choosing yourself. Thank you for saying yes to your healing. Thank you for letting me walk with you on this journey.

You are not alone. You were never broken. And I am honored to be part of your becoming.

ABOUT THE AUTHOR

Jennifer A. Matwawana

Jennifer A. Matwawana is an award-winning speaker, therapist, educator, entrepreneur, and emotional intelligence expert with more than 27 years of experience helping people reclaim their power, strengthen their confidence, and transform their lives from the inside out.

Jennifer is the co-founder of AWL Partners, the parent company behind All Women L.E.A.D.®, a global leadership community that empowers women and allies through workshops, conferences, coaching, counseling, and executive development. She is also the creator of the popular programs Slay Your Inner Critic and the J.A.M. Effect™, both rooted in emotional intelligence, self-leadership, and intentional living.

A Registered Social Worker by training, Jennifer has supported individuals, families, organizations, and entire communities through her work in child welfare, psychotherapy, leadership development, equity and inclusion, and trauma-informed practice. She is known for her ability to blend humor, storytelling, and science into powerful learning experiences that resonate with audiences worldwide.

Her work has earned her multiple honors, including the Queen Elizabeth II Diamond Jubilee Award, the City of London Diversity, Inclusion and Anti-Oppression Award, and the King's University College Alumni Award of Distinction. She has delivered keynote talks and trainings for major institutions such as TD, Fanshawe College, Lerners LLP, Western University, and organizations across Canada and internationally.

Jennifer is also a co-creator of the anti-racism education series Shifting Perspectives and the award-winning television program Melanated View.

Known for her authenticity, warmth, and ability to "say the hard things gently," Jennifer invites people to step into self-awareness, emotional regulation, confidence, and purpose. Her work blends neuroscience, psychology, lived experience, and deep compassion, helping people not just understand themselves, but choose themselves.

Jennifer lives in Ottawa with her husband and proudly celebrates her blended family of five adult children and their beautiful families. This book reflects her deepest belief:

"When you learn to lead your inner world, your outer world transforms."

Table of Contents

Prelude 1

How To Read This Book.. 8

Introduction 15

Part I Journey & Awareness

Chapter One The Moment You Hear Yourself: Awareness Begins 21

Chapter Two The Inner Critic: Who's Really Talking? 43

Chapter Three The Subconscious Code: How Your Past Writes Your Present .. 58

Chapter Four Schemas, Shadism, And Survival: The Lenses 71

Chapter Five The Comfort Zone & The Lie Of Safety 83

Part II Mastery

Chapter Six Emotional Intelligence: The Skill That Changes Everything 98

Chapter Seven Rewriting Your Script: The P.A.I.D. Method™ 116

Chapter Eight From Self-Doubt To Self-Trust: The T.A.G. Method™ 129

Chapter Nine Perfectionism, Procrastination, & The Frozen Self.................... 141

Chapter Ten The I Hate Exercise: Transforming Your Triggers 158

Chapter Eleven Thought Records For Real Life (Not Therapy Rooms) 175

Chapter Twelve Boundaries, Beliefs, And Becoming 189

Part III Momentum

Chapter Thirteen Fear (Part 1): How It Traps You 206

Chapter Fourteen Fear (Part 2): How You Break Through 221

Chapter Fifteen Forgiveness (Part 1): The Wound Beneath The Critic 234

Chapter Sixteen Forgiveness (Part 2): Freedom Through Release 253

Chapter Seventeen The Six Areas Of Life: Where Your Critic Lives 270

Chapter Eighteen "Energy, Alignment, And The Happy Life 292

Conclusion The J.A.M. Effect™ In Full: Choosing Your Life, Every Day 311

Interviews 318

PRELUDE

Before the Critic Had a Name

My Journey to the J.A.M. Effect™

Let me start with the truth:

I didn't write this book because I mastered my inner critic. I wrote it because I survived her.

And if you're holding this book, I'm willing to bet you've survived yours too. Maybe you still battle her every day. Maybe you've just discovered that quiet, persistent voice running in the background of your life. Maybe you're exhausted from being brave for everyone else.

Wherever you are in your journey, I see you because I was you.

Growing Up In The In-Between

I was born in Thompson, Manitoba, a nickel mining town of about 20,000 people, with only 50 to 75 Black folks in the whole community. My Jamaican parents were educators, and I lived my entire childhood in the "in-between":

- too light-skinned for some

- too outspoken for others

- too talented to blend in

- too different to belong anywhere

I fit in with everyone… which meant I fit in with no one.

Shadism from some Black girls. Curiosity from White folks. And a constant sense of being observed, evaluated, misunderstood.

That's where the earliest seeds of my inner critic were planted, long before I had a name for her.

Talent Doesn't Protect You From Shame

I excelled at almost everything, sports, music, academics, but talent doesn't shield you from identity wounds. If anything, it adds pressure. When adults told me, "You have so much potential," I heard:

"You better not mess this up."

"You're already behind."

"You're one mistake away from disappointing everyone."

So, I became a people-pleaser, especially with boys. Validation became oxygen.

The Detour That Felt Like Failure

At 19, I entered a serious relationship. At 22, I had an unplanned pregnancy.

Even though I made the Dean's List while pregnant and raising an infant, I felt nothing but shame. I had broken the "rules" I believed proved I was a good woman:

school

degree

career

marriage

home

then children

I was doing everything "backwards," and my inner critic had a field day.

She told me I had disappointed my parents.

She told me I lacked discipline.

She told me medical school had never been right for me because I wasn't right for it.

Her voice became a constant soundtrack.

Marriage, Motherhood, And The Loudest Version Of My Critic

I eventually married someone else and had two more beautiful children, but a strong family can't grow on a foundation of self-doubt.

When you don't love yourself, you choose from fear.

When you don't know yourself, you repeat patterns instead of choosing partners.

Suspected infidelity.

My own affair in response.

A painful divorce.

And my critic's voice was screaming louder than ever.

It was so dark at one point that I wondered if my absence would be easier for everyone else, or maybe easier for me.

My Promise To God

In that moment, I whispered a promise:

"If You get me through this, I will spend my life helping others manage the voice trying to destroy them."

God kept His promise.

So now, I keep mine.

Rebuilding, Rewiring, Reclaiming

I spent years studying myself, my patterns, triggers, childhood conditioning, emotional intelligence, and the subconscious stories shaping my confidence. I intentionally built a circle of women who spoke love over me until I could speak love over myself.

I mothered myself.

I forgave myself.

I rebuilt myself.

And today, I am married to a man who sees me, loves me, and meets me as an equal. My children are thriving. And although life isn't perfect, it is beautiful and it is mine.

Where The J.A.M. Effect™ Was Born

People assume frameworks are born in boardrooms. But the J.A.M. Effect wasn't created at a whiteboard. It was shaped in my lived experience, in years of hesitation, healing, and spiritual preparation.

Three years ago, this book was supposed to be finished. I had the interviews. I had the research. We had perfected our Slay Your Inner Critic course.

But something in me wouldn't move forward. At the time, I thought it was procrastination. Now I know it was alignment.

I was practicing the method without yet knowing its name. Over those years, I kept noticing, naming, reframing, and repeating the exact process that would one day become the J.A.M. Effect. I was living it long before I could articulate it.

Then, in October 2025, I married the love of my life and took my new name:

Jennifer Adrienne Matwawana.

And suddenly, the method snapped into place:

J = Judgment-Free Awareness

A = Aligned Action

M = Momentum Through Self-Mastery

It was my whole life, my early wounds, my mistakes, my healing, my faith, my training, crystallized into a simple, powerful framework that explained how I rose.

The book wasn't late.

The method wasn't late.

I wasn't late.

Everything became clear at the exact moment I became the woman ready to own it.

Why I'm Telling You This

Because you are not broken: you are patterned. And patterns can be changed.

Your inner critic is not the truth: she is a story. And stories can be rewritten.

Let's begin.

HOW TO READ THIS BOOK

A Guide for Your Journey

Before you go any further, I encourage you to pause for a moment and take a breath.

This book is not meant to be read the way you've read most books. This is not a book you "get through." It's a book you experience.

Every chapter, every story, every pull quote, every exercise, every affirmation is here for a reason: to help you shift from surviving your inner critic to mastering your inner voice.

This book was written for you. For your healing, your clarity, your strength, and your becoming.

My deepest hope is that you don't just read these words, but you let them work in you.

Here's how to get the most out of this journey:

1. Read Slowly. This Is Not a Race.

You will see stories. You will see truths that might sting. You will see yourself.

Don't rush through that. Permit yourself to put the book down, journal, cry, breathe, or simply sit quietly with a moment that touches something tender.

Your healing is not meant to be hurried.

2. Use the Affirmations as Tools, Not Decor.

Throughout the book, you'll find affirmations: sentences designed to retrain your subconscious and rewire your emotional patterns. They are not filler. They are medicine.

Copy them. Write them on sticky notes. Put them on your mirror, your phone wallpaper, your walls, your journal, your vision board. Basically anywhere your eyes land every day.

Say them out loud until they feel less foreign and more familiar. These affirmations help you do the internal rewiring your critic has been undoing for years. They are permission in sentence form.

3. Let the Pull Quotes Interrupt You.

The pull quotes are invitations. They are meant to stop you mid-sentence and make you think. Some will challenge you. Some will comfort you. Some will call you out lovingly.

Sit with them. Ask yourself: Why did this hit me the way it did? What truth is it trying to show me?

Reflection is where insight becomes transformation.

4. Engage Fully With the Exercises.

This book includes exercises designed to help you understand your patterns, interrupt your critic, rewrite your subconscious scripts, build emotional intelligence, reimagine your future, and reconnect with your voice.

Don't skip them. You can read stories all day long, but transformation requires application. This book becomes powerful when you do the work.

5. Let the Stories and the Interviews Be Mirrors.

You will meet real people in these pages: clients, students, children, adults, and versions of myself I have grown through. And at the end of the book, you will meet real people who generously shared their journeys.

These stories and interviews are not there to entertain you. They are there to remind you that you are not alone.

Stories teach us compassion. Interviews show us the possibility. Both help you see your own humanity more clearly.

6. Take This Book in Stages if You Need To.

This is a "come back to it" book. Some chapters may ask more of you than you feel ready for, and that is okay.

If you need time, take it. If you need space, honor it. If you need safety, seek it. Healing has no deadline.

7. Keep a Notebook Close By.

You will want space to reflect, write your truths, capture your insights, process your emotions, challenge your critic, and celebrate your breakthroughs.

Think of this book as a guide, and your notebook as the place where the guide becomes your way.

8. Read With Compassion, Not Judgment.

As you go deeper into your subconscious, childhood patterns, emotional triggers, and survival strategies, you may feel shame rising. You may think: "I should have known better." "I should have healed this by now." "I shouldn't still be dealing with this."

Pause. You were doing the best you could with the emotional tools you had. Now you're learning new ones.

Compassion opens doors that judgment will always close.

9. Let This Be a Conversation With Yourself.

As you read, notice your reactions. What makes you nod? What makes you uncomfortable? What makes you emotional? What makes you defensive? What makes you hopeful?

Those reactions are data. They're part of your healing. Let them speak.

Because this book isn't just a collection of chapters: it's an invitation to hear your own voice again.

10. Understand One Thing: This Book Was Written for Your Becoming.

Every exercise, every framework, every affirmation, every story, every pull quote, and every chapter was created to support your healing, your growth, and your alignment. You are not reading this book by accident.

This book is for the part of you that knows there is more for your life… and is finally ready to meet the version of you who rises.

Take your time.

Do the work.

Let yourself expand.

Let yourself be transformed.

And most of all, let yourself be free.

A Gentle Note On Support

As you move through this book, some of the stories, reflections, and exercises may bring up emotions, memories, or reactions that feel intense or difficult to manage on your own. This is a natural part of growth and healing, and it's nothing to be ashamed of.

You are not meant to do this work in isolation.

If at any point you feel overwhelmed, stuck, or unsure how to process what's coming up, I strongly encourage you to reach out to a counselor, therapist, coach, or other trusted support professional. Having someone to debrief with, reflect alongside, and help you make meaning of your experience can deepen the work and keep you grounded.

Support is not a sign of weakness. It is a sign of self-respect.

Take care of yourself as you read. Move at your own pace. Pause when needed. And remember: you deserve to be held with the same compassion you are learning to offer yourself.

INTRODUCTION

The Promise I Made to God

From Breaking Point to Becoming

"At some point, you get tired of fighting battles you were never meant to fight alone."

As mentioned, I didn't set out to write a book about the inner critic. I set out to survive her.

I set out to finally understand the voice that had been whispering in my ear for decades: sometimes softly, sometimes brutally, shaping how I saw myself, how I moved through the world, and how I loved, worked, parented, performed, and hid.

That voice didn't start in adulthood. It started long before I had language for it.

Growing up in Thompson, Manitoba, my earliest memories held both beauty and bewilderment. I was a bubbly little girl with bright brown eyes and big energy, but even then, something in me knew that the world had already drawn conclusions about me that I didn't yet understand.

I grew up navigating shadism, invisibility, unwanted attention, and the complicated truth that being seen was both a risk and a longing. I learned early how to shrink, how to smile through discomfort, how to earn affection, and how to disappear when needed. I learned how to carry other people's projections, fears, judgments, and desires on a body that was still learning itself.

And like so many girls, especially Black girls, I internalized it.

I believed that something about me needed fixing. Softened. Muted. Managed. Perfected. Controlled.

I didn't know then that I was forming a relationship with my inner critic, a voice that would grow louder, sharper, more sophisticated as I navigated school, relationships, career, motherhood, and marriage.

I didn't know that this voice would shape my choices, my boundaries, my confidence, and my sense of worth in ways that felt normal at the time... until they nearly broke me.

The Breaking Point

There came a moment, one of those quiet, private moments that no one sees, when I found myself exhausted. Not physically, though my body was tired. Not mentally, though my mind was crowded. I was spiritually exhausted.

I was tired of performing strength, pretending I was fine, over-functioning, absorbing disrespect, rescuing everyone but myself, ignoring my own intuition, living inside a life that looked good from the outside but didn't nourish me on the inside.

I reached a point where I couldn't keep pushing. Something had to give, and it couldn't be me anymore.

So, I prayed a prayer that would change everything.

"God, if You bring me through and help me really know my worth, I promise to help others get through their hard times and learn to understand their worth, too."

I didn't know what I was asking for. I didn't realize that seeing myself would mean unlearning almost everything I'd been taught to believe. I didn't understand yet that healing would require confronting wounds I buried, facing fears I justified, releasing patterns I normalized, forgiving people who never apologized, and forgiving myself for not knowing what I know now.

I didn't yet know that the journey back to myself would require courage, honesty, humility, and emotional intelligence.

But I made a promise, and God held me to it.

The Turning Point: Awareness

As a therapist, leader, and speaker, I have supported countless people through their deepest struggles. But there is a difference between holding space for others and holding truth for yourself.

My turning point didn't come through a dramatic moment. It came through awareness: quiet, persistent, convicting awareness.

Awareness that the voice criticizing my every move wasn't wisdom.

Awareness that the guilt I carried wasn't mine.

Awareness that the patterns I repeated weren't destiny.

Awareness that the life I was living wasn't aligned with the woman I was becoming.

It was during this season that I realized something essential:

"Your inner critic is not your enemy. She is your unhealed story trying to protect you."

Once I understood that, everything changed.

I learned emotional intelligence not just as a concept, but as a way of life: emotional regulation, self-awareness, boundaries, self-trust, compassion, alignment.

I learned to make choices from truth rather than fear. I learned how to lead myself. And eventually, I learned how to silence the critic and amplify the voice of the woman I was always meant to be.

I know what it feels like to doubt yourself, overthink everything, perform for acceptance, carry generational expectations, lose yourself in relationships, apologize for existing, silence your dreams, fear success, and question your worth.

And I know what it feels like to rise.

I wrote this book because the world doesn't need more perfect women. The world needs more women who are self-aware, emotionally intelligent, and aligned.

Women who know how to regulate instead of react, respond instead of retreat, speak instead of shrink, forgive instead of freeze, choose instead of chase.

This book is not a theory. It is a roadmap.

A roadmap back to yourself.

A Promise To You

My promise to you is the same promise I made to God:

I will tell the truth. Not the polished truth, not the rehearsed truth, not the professional truth, but the real truth.

I will walk with you through the hard places: the wounds, the fear, the shame, the anger, the forgiveness, the boundaries, the freedom.

I will teach you the tools that helped me reclaim my life. I will share the stories that shaped me. I will give you everything I know about emotional intelligence, healing, patterns, confidence, power, and peace.

And by the time you reach the end of this book, I hope you hear your own voice again, or maybe for the first time: clearly, confidently, compassionately, because that is the voice that will lead you into the future you deserve.

CHAPTER ONE

The Moment You Hear Yourself

Awareness Begins

"You can't hit your mark on a dartboard if you throw darts in the dark."

Let's start here: how well do you really know yourself?

That's not a rhetorical question, I mean it. When you get anxious, do you recognize the signs? When you lash out at someone, can you name the feeling underneath? When you succeed, do you pause and fully take it in, or do you move right past it?

That's what awareness is. And it's a game-changer.

We hear the word 'awareness' all the time. Self-awareness. Mindfulness. But what does it really mean?

The textbook answer goes something like this: awareness is the knowledge or perception of a situation or a fact. Self-awareness, then, is the ability to accurately perceive your own emotions in the moment and understand your tendencies across different situations.

Ready to ask yourself a question and reflect?

Here we go…

What's the worst thing you've ever said to yourself?

Not out loud, but those quiet, under-your-breath thoughts. The ones no one else hears… but you do. Loud and clear.

We all have an inner voice. But for many of us, that voice is less "motivational life coach" and more "grumpy old critic with a megaphone." It says things like:

- "You're not good enough."

- "Who do you think you are?"

- "You're too much."

- "You're not enough."

That voice might sound like yours, but it isn't really you. Not the real you.

I call it the Inner Critic. And if left unchecked, it can shape how you show up in your relationships, your leadership, your parenting, your career, and your sense of self-worth.

There was a time when I didn't even realize I had an inner critic. I thought the things I said to myself were just… facts. If I wasn't reaching my goals fast enough, it was because I was lazy. If I made a mistake, I must have been incompetent. If I had a brilliant idea, I'd shut it down before it had a chance to grow.

I internalized every harsh word spoken to me throughout my life and unknowingly gave that voice a home. I furnished it, gave it a comfortable seat, and let it dictate my thoughts. But here's what I learned as a therapist, a coach, and a woman who has done the deep work:

That voice is not the truth.

It's a mix of fear, old wounds, cultural conditioning, generational messaging, and stories we picked up along the way. And while it may never disappear completely, we can turn down its volume and amplify something far more powerful: our inner wisdom.

That's where awareness begins.

That's where your life starts to shift.

Awareness Is A Choice

Let me ask you something real.

How well do you actually know yourself?

When you get anxious, do you recognize the signs?

When you lash out, do you know the feeling underneath?

When you succeed, do you pause and receive it, or rush past it?

Awareness is not passive. It's intentional. It's choosing to notice what's happening inside of you before reacting to what's happening outside of you.

For years, I thought I was self-aware because I was "doing the work." I taught emotional intelligence, facilitated workshops, and supported others in their growth. And then I entered a coaching program to help me grow AWL Partners. The goal was business expansion and creativity, but what it gave me was unexpected:

Stillness. Reflection. Presence.

Slowing down brought a level of awareness I didn't know I needed. And that's when I realized:

Awareness is not a destination.

It is a discipline.

Emotions Have A Purpose

Every emotion you feel is communicating something.

Fear says: "Be careful. Something feels unsafe."

Sadness says: "You've lost something important."

Anger says: "A boundary has been violated."

Emotions are not the enemy. They're information. Awareness helps you decode that information instead of being controlled by it.

Case Study: Jillian's Speech

Jillian was a tenth-grade student paralyzed by public speaking. Before presentations, she'd become irritable and snappy with her friends. They pulled away, assuming she had a bad attitude.

Before her third speech, a friend gently pointed out the pattern. Jillian paused long enough for awareness to do its job. She realized her irritability wasn't "bad attitude"; it was fear.

That moment of awareness gave her a choice.

Before, she was just reacting. But now that she could name what was happening, she had the power to shift how she handled stress.

What About The Inner Critic?

Let's bring it back to the voice in your head. Some people believe the inner critic should be silenced entirely because it's negative. But here's what I've learned: sometimes, the critic has a point.

Sometimes, it's alerting us to risk. Sometimes, it's reflecting something we've avoided dealing with. The problem isn't always what it says; it's that we:

- Avoid listening too closely

- Distract ourselves so we don't have to think

- Obsess over the message until we're paralyzed

And that paralysis? It keeps us playing small. It makes us choose not to show up fully. Yes, I said choose. We'll come back to that.

This book is here to help you manage your critic, not ignore it, not let it run wild, but manage it. You'll get tools, stories, and strategies to help you decide just how much space that voice gets in your life.

But first, we need to understand the systems that shape your awareness. Because, believe it or not, the way your brain is wired plays a huge role in how you hear and respond to your inner critic.

Awareness moves me from reaction to intention.

The Inner Critic: Who's Really Talking?

Now that you understand awareness, let's talk about the voice that challenges it.

The inner critic is not an audible voice; it's the stream of thoughts that judge, shame, and limit you. Psychologists sometimes call it the "anti-self."

Some call it:

- The Judge

- The Gremlin

- The Saboteur

- The Mean Girl

- The Inner Bully

- The Peanut Gallery

Call it whatever you like, but its function is generally the same: to keep you safe by keeping you small.

A Bully In Disguise

Let's talk about bullies.

Do you remember the bully from your childhood? The one who teased others on the playground, who controlled through fear? Maybe you were the one being bullied? Maybe, if you're brave enough to admit it, you were the one doing the bullying?

Either way, bullies don't come from nowhere. They often act out of fear: fear of not being in control, of being hurt first, of being seen as weak. The inner critic is no different.

It may sound harsh, even cruel.

But what it's often trying to say is: "I don't want you to get hurt again."

It tries to protect you by limiting you.

Think about it. When you're about to step out of your comfort zone, does your inner critic whisper things like:

- "People are going to laugh at you."

- "You'll fail again."

- "Who do you think you are?"

That's not the truth. That's a fear-based protection strategy. One that, ironically, ends up hurting us more than it helps.

That's protection masquerading as logic.

The Story Of Sam

I once worked with a ten-year-old boy, let's call him Sam.

From the outside, Sam looked like your average kid: wide brown eyes, quick to smile, curious. But it didn't take long to realize that he was carrying an emotional weight, one no child should have to hold.

He was emotionally intuitive, deeply sensitive, and remarkably attuned to others' feelings. In session, I'd see him shift in his seat whenever something difficult came up, his body tightening, his face hardening, like he was preparing for battle. A battle inside himself.

One day, during a particularly emotional moment, I watched his eyes well up with tears. His lip trembled, but instead of letting the tears fall, he inhaled sharply, clenched his fists, and whispered:

"I'm fine. I'm not gonna cry."

I paused. "Why not?"

Sam looked at the floor. His voice barely audible, he answered:

"He says I'm weak. I'm not allowed to be weak."

"He" was Sam's father. A man who had grown up in an era, and likely in an environment, where emotions were considered dangerous, feminine, and unwelcome. A "boys don't cry" kind of man. A "suck it up and deal with it" kind of man. He wasn't trying to be cruel; in his mind, he was preparing Sam for the real world. He thought he was protecting his son.

But instead, Sam was learning to suppress his natural emotions. He wasn't speaking in his own voice; he was repeating someone else's script. One that taught him that vulnerability was weakness, and that expressing emotion would make him less of a boy… and by extension, less of a person.

Just like many of us.

Maybe someone told you that you were "too much," or "too loud," or "too sensitive," or "too ambitious," or "too emotional," or "too quiet," or "not enough."

And somewhere along the way, you believed them.

"Be careful whose voice becomes your conscience."

The Science Behind The Critic

Let's break this down a bit.

Your brain is wired for survival, not happiness. Its number one job? Keep you safe. Not successful. Not bold. Not fulfilled. Just… safe.

When you hear the inner critic, it's often your brain's way of avoiding what it perceives as danger: embarrassment, failure, rejection, judgment.

And here's the twist: the inner critic doesn't just yell insults. Sometimes it whispers reasonable-sounding things, like:

- "Let's wait until we have more experience."

- "Now's not the right time."

- "We just want to be realistic."

Sound familiar? It's called rationalization, and it's a favorite tool of the inner critic. It makes fear feel like logic.

When Protection Becomes Prison

Imagine you're at a sleepover as a kid. You're excited. Nervous. But when bedtime comes, you suddenly feel sick, anxious, uncertain. You want to go home.

You call your mom, and she picks you up. You feel safe again. Crisis averted.

Fast forward to adulthood.

Every time you feel uncertain or emotionally uncomfortable, your brain remembers that going home felt safe. Except now "safe" might mean not applying for that job. Or not telling someone how you really feel. Or not showing up as your full self.

And the inner critic reinforces that choice. It tells you:

- "Don't rock the boat."

- "You're being dramatic."

- "Better to stay quiet."

That's the same protective instinct.

But now? It's keeping you stuck.

When the Critic Wears a Mask

Sometimes the inner critic doesn't sound like a bully. Sometimes… it sounds helpful.

It's cautious.

It's logical.

It even sounds smart.

But here's what I've learned, both in my own healing and in coaching hundreds of others:

The inner critic doesn't need to be loud to be dangerous. Sometimes the softest voices cause the deepest hesitation.

And often, it's perfectionism wearing a disguise.

When Perfection Becomes a Prison

Perfectionism tells us that if we just do everything right, no one can judge us. No one can criticize us. No one can abandon us.

But in the chase for "right," we often lose sight of real.

We perform instead of participating.

We analyze instead of acting.

We plan… and plan… and plan, until the moment's passed.

And the inner critic? It loves it when you stay frozen.

Because frozen means safe.

Frozen means no risk of embarrassment.

Frozen means no growth, no healing, no joy. But also… no life.

"Perfectionism is not a standard. It is a shield."

— Brené Brown

Where The Critic Began

Nobody is born hating themselves.

Nobody enters the world thinking they're not enough.

So, where does the inner critic come from? Sometimes:

- A teacher told you your idea was stupid.

- A parent constantly corrected your tone, weight, posture, or grammar.

- A friend once said you were "too much," and you decided to shrink ever since.

- A society taught you that your body, your hair, your accent, your skin, your ambition, your softness, your tears were wrong.

And just like that, a voice was planted.

You didn't ask for it. But you rehearsed it over and over until it became automatic.

Now?

It lives in your brain, uninvited but familiar. Running your thoughts. Shaping your actions. Pretending to be your own voice.

The Ras: Your Brain's Filter System

Naming the Voice

One of the most powerful things you can do is this:

Give the critic a name.

Not your name. Not you.

A name that reminds you it's separate from your truth.

Some of my clients named theirs:

- "Bossy Brenda"

- "Doubtful Dan"

- "The Peanut Gallery"

- "Fear Voice"

- "My Dad's Ghost"

You don't have to be clever. You just have to be clear.

Because once you name it, you create distance. And from that distance, you can finally choose whether to listen… or to lead.

Reflect & Write

Try this short exercise before we move on:

1. What is one sentence your inner critic says often?

e.g., "You're going to mess this up," "They're going to judge you," "You're not qualified."

2. Whose voice does it remind you of?

A parent, a teacher, an ex, an institution, yourself?

3. Give your inner critic a name.

Make it specific. Silly is okay. Honest is better.

Next time it speaks, say: "Thank you for trying to protect me [insert name], but I choose truth instead."

Rewiring Your Filters: The RAS in Action

"You see what your brain wants you to see."

There's a system in your brain called the Reticular Activating System, or RAS for short.

It's not a concept I invented. It's neuroscience.

And it's the same brain system responsible for why you suddenly notice a million red cars after you decide to buy a red car. Or why, after a breakup, every song on the radio feels like it was written specifically to ruin your life.

That's your RAS at work. It filters the millions of bits of data your brain receives every second. But here's the kicker:

Your RAS doesn't choose what's "true." It chooses what aligns with your beliefs.

So if your inner critic is whispering "You're not smart enough," "You're not ready," or "People will reject you," your RAS will find evidence to support that belief. Not because it's true. But because it's familiar.

The Lens of Confirmation

Let's say you walk into a team meeting. You share a suggestion, and one person looks down at their phone.

If your belief is "No one takes me seriously," your RAS files that phone glance as proof. But if your belief is "My ideas have value," your RAS notices the three people leaning forward.

Same moment. Different interpretation. Radically different experience.

"Change the way you look at things, and the things you look at change."

— Wayne Dyer

The good news? You can retrain your RAS. Just like you trained it before, only this time, with intention.

Here's how to start:

1. Identify the belief your inner critic is promoting.

2. Challenge it with evidence.

What moments prove the opposite? What small wins have you overlooked?

3. Replace it with a new belief, one that is still believable.

Not toxic positivity. Not unicorn rainbows. Something grounded and real.

4. Prime your RAS.

Every morning or before a meeting, say the belief out loud. Write it down. Repeat it. Visualize it. Your RAS takes repetition as instruction.

A Quick Reset Ritual: The 3 R's

Here's a tool you can use in-the-moment when your critic flares up:

The 3 R's For Reframing

- **Recognize** the thought. Is it fear? Judgment? Doubt? Name it: "This is my critic speaking."

- **Reframe** the belief. Replace it with something supportive and true.

- **Repeat** the reframe. In your mind. Out loud. On paper. The more you repeat, the more your RAS listens.

"Recognize the thought. Reframe the belief. Repeat the new truth."

You're not broken. You're practiced.

You've practiced hearing the critic for years. Now it's time to practice hearing your truth.

Because underneath all the noise and conditioning, there's a voice that believes in you. A voice that's been whispering all along:

That voice is yours. Let's find it again.

Where Is Your Inner Critic the Loudest?

As you deepen your awareness, it helps to notice where your critic tends to surface most often. For most people, it's not everywhere; it's specific.

Try reflecting on these six areas of your life:

Career: Does your critic speak up around success, promotion, or leadership?

Finances: Is it telling you you're irresponsible, behind, or incapable?

Relationships: Does it sabotage your self-worth or how you show up with others?

Health: Is there guilt, shame, or comparison?

Spirituality: Are you disconnected from your inner compass or doubting it?

Personal Growth: Are you stuck in old patterns instead of choosing new paths?

You'll see these six areas pop up again in later chapters, which offer space to reflect more deeply. For now, just notice where the volume is loudest.

I am not the voice of my inner critic. I am the voice of my healing.

I hear the voice. But I do not have to obey it.

I train my brain to see what serves me, not what scares me.

CHAPTER TWO

The Inner Critic

Who's Really Talking?

"Your lens is not your identity. It is simply the story your past told your brain."

The Quietest Voice With The Loudest Impact

When was the last time you stopped yourself from doing something you really wanted to do? Not because you couldn't, but because a voice inside whispered:

- "You're not ready."

- "You're not enough."

- "You'll embarrass yourself."

- "People will judge you."

That voice is your inner critic. Every one of us has one. No exceptions.

No matter how successful, beautiful, intelligent, or accomplished you are, if you're human, you have heard it.

But here's the truth we forget:

The inner critic is not the truth. It's a story. A script. A collection of fears wrapped in a tone that sounds like you.

If you take nothing else from this chapter, take this:

You are not the voice inside your head. You are the one listening to it.

Where The Critic Comes From

Nobody is born doubting themselves. Babies don't come into the world thinking they're "too much," "not enough," or "unworthy." So where does it come from?

Usually from one of these places:

A Parent's Voice

Sometimes it's loud and harsh.

Sometimes it's quiet but consistent.

"Stop crying."

"Fix your face."

"You're too sensitive."

"Don't embarrass us."

Even well-intentioned parents can accidentally plant seeds that grow into entire internal belief systems.

A Teacher's Words

A single sentence said at the wrong time can become a lifelong narrative.

"You talk too much."

"You need to calm down."

"You're not leadership material."

Culture

Gender norms.

Racial stereotypes.

Beauty standards.

Accent discrimination.

Expectations around behavior, tone, ambition, weight, and hair.

These messages shape us long before we realize they've shaped us.

A Past Hurt

Heartbreak.

Failure.

Rejection.

Humiliation. Loss.

The critic stores these moments like evidence and brings them up whenever you try to grow.

Survival

Sometimes the critic is the voice you built to stay safe, especially in homes or communities where vulnerability wasn't welcome.

And the most frustrating truth?

We didn't ask for these voices… but we rehearsed them until they sounded like our own.

In Chapter 1, we explored how early experiences shape our emotional blueprint. Here, we go deeper: your inner critic is often the emotional residue of those moments, fossilized into thoughts.

A Story: When Playfulness Met A Label

When I was a kid, I was rambunctious. I loved to play, to jump, to run, whether we were indoors or not. I once went to a sleepover and did all of those things. I had fun. I was being myself. But after that sleepover, one of my girlfriends pulled me aside and told me something that made my heart drop.

"One of the parents called you a 'bitch on wheels.'"

Oof.

That hurt. A lot.

But it was also the beginning. The beginning of hearing others' voices as my critics. That one comment stuck, not because it was true, but because it echoed a pattern I'd already started to notice. The rolling eyes of adults when I entered a room. The disapproving sighs. I wasn't the docile, sweet little Jamaican girl I was supposed to be.

I was loud. Energetic. Enthusiastic. Alive. And apparently, that needed to be quieted.

That's how it starts for so many of us. The critic doesn't arrive full-formed. It's built over time, piece by piece, from comments, reactions, exclusions, expectations. Until one day, it sounds like us.

The True Purpose Of The Inner Critic

The critic's job is simple:

Keep you safe. By keeping you small.

It's not trying to ruin your life. It's not trying to hurt you. It's trying to protect you from:

- embarrassment

- disappointment

- rejection

- failure

- judgment

But protection becomes prison when it stops you from living.

Think about how your critic speaks when you want to:

- apply for a promotion

- start a business

- publish your art

- tell someone how you really feel

- set a boundary

- leave a situation

- choose peace

- choose yourself

It whispers:

- "Let's wait."

- "Let's be realistic."

- "Don't get ahead of yourself."

- "What if you fail?"

That's not logic. That's fear wearing a business suit.

The Brain Science Behind Your Critic

Your brain is wired for survival, not success. Its job is not to help you shine. Its job is to help you avoid threats.

Here's the trick. Your brain registers criticism, rejection, embarrassment, judgment, and failure as threats. So the inner critic speaks up whenever growth feels risky. It doesn't care that you want to expand. It cares that you might get hurt.

And to your brain, hurt equals danger.

Neuroscience Insight:

The amygdala, the brain's threat detector, triggers your fear response before your prefrontal cortex (your rational brain) can intervene. That's why the critic often shows up first, loud and fast, before logic gets a chance to speak.

But here's the good news: awareness slows this process down. Mindfulness, journaling, and Emotional Intelligence (EQ) all activate your brain's regulatory systems, calming the amygdala and engaging the prefrontal cortex. That's when you can begin to choose a new response.

When The Critic Sounds "Reasonable"

Not every critic is loud. Some are soft, polished, and professional-sounding. These say things like:

- "We just need more time."

- "Let's be realistic."

- "Maybe next year."

- "I'm not ready."

- "People like me don't do things like that."

These critics don't scream. They negotiate you out of your own greatness. They keep you calm. Small. Predictable.

But here's the truth:

You cannot step into a life you want while obeying a voice designed to protect you from the life you have.

Perfectionism: The Critic's Favorite Mask

Perfectionism tells you: "If I get everything right, no one can judge me."

But the cost is enormous.

You plan instead of acting.

You rehearse instead of showing up.

You analyze instead of choosing. You freeze.

And frozen feels safe. But it is not living.

Perfectionism doesn't protect you from criticism. It protects you from growth.

The Critic Thrives In Silence

The critic grows strongest when:

- You never question it

- You never speak back

- You never name it

- You never interrupt its stories

Awareness is the beginning of change. Which is why one of the most powerful steps you can take is this:

Give your critic a name.

Mine has been called many things over the years. Some of my clients named theirs:

- Bossy Brenda

- Doubtful Dan

- The Peanut Gallery

- Birtha

- That Gym Teacher

- My Mother-In-Law's Ghost

- The Boardroom Bully

It doesn't have to be clever. Just separate enough from you to remind you:

This voice is not your identity. It's a pattern. And patterns can be changed.

Revisiting The Reticular Activating System (Ras): Your Brain's Filter

Your brain filters millions of pieces of information every second. It filters based on what you believe.

If your belief is "I'm not good enough," your RAS will look for proof.

If your belief is "I deserve to grow," your RAS will find possibilities.

This chapter will help you begin to interrupt, challenge, and rewrite the beliefs your critic feeds your RAS.

When you change the belief, you change the evidence.

When you change the evidence, you change the story.

When you change the story, you change your life.

Reflection Exercise: Meet Your Critic

Take a moment and write down:

1. What is one sentence your critic says often? What's its favorite script?

2. Whose voice does it sound like?

A parent? A teacher? Someone from your past?

3. What name will you give it?

Silly names work. Honest names work better.

4. What does this voice pretend to protect you from?

Judgment? Failure? Being seen?

This first step, naming your critic, is the doorway to reclaiming your power.

Affirmations For Reclaiming Your Voice

I hear the voice, but I choose the truth.

I am growing beyond the limits of my past.

I am learning to trust myself again.

**I am not the voice of my inner critic. I am the
voice of my healing.**

"Be careful whose voice becomes your conscience."

— Unknown

"Your inner critic is loudest when you're closest to growth."

— J.M.

"Healing begins where silence ends."

— J.M.

You Are Not Alone

If you're reading this and recognizing your own patterns, good.
That's where the shift begins.

But don't try to do it alone. Support is out there. Be intentional about finding, accessing, and using it. Whether through a coach, a therapist, a mentor, a group, or a friend, your healing deserves a witness.

And your voice deserves the microphone.

You are not the voice of your inner critic. You are the author of your next chapter.

CHAPTER THREE

The Subconscious Code

How Your Past Writes Your Present

"If you want to change your life, you have first to change your mind."

You are not broken; you are practiced.

And nothing gets more practice than your subconscious mind.

This chapter is about understanding the code that has been quietly running in the background of your life: the automatic thoughts, reflexes, triggers, and assumptions you didn't choose, but inherited, absorbed, learned, and repeated.

Once you understand this code, you can finally rewrite it.

Are You Running On Autopilot?

Pause for a moment and ask yourself something real: Why do I think the way I think?

Not what you think, but why.

Why do you assume you're unqualified before you apply? Brace for the worst, even when nothing is wrong? Feel uncomfortable when someone compliments you? Expect rejection before you even walk into the room?

Here's the truth most people never learn:

You weren't born thinking this way. You were trained.

Trained by experience.

Trained by family dynamics.

Trained by culture.

Trained by pain.

Trained by the voices you absorbed long before you had one of your own.

And most of that training happened below the surface, in the place where habits, fears, and beliefs form without permission.

Your inner critic isn't a personality flaw. It's a subconscious program. A script written without your consent.

This chapter helps you expose the script, so you can finally take the pen back.

The Mind Beneath The Mind

Most people believe they control their thoughts.

But neuroscience and real life tell a different story.

Only 5 to 10% of your mind is conscious.

The other 90 to 95% is like a silent puppeteer pulling the strings.

Your habits

Your assumptions

Your emotional triggers

Your fear responses

Your automatic reactions

Your beliefs about your worth

Most of your behavior is being guided by a system you rarely think about, a system programmed long ago.

Think of your brain like a computer.

On the surface, you, the user, are working on a document, browsing the web, maybe watching a video.

But beneath the surface? There are dozens of background processes running at once: firewalls, auto-updates, virus scans, syncing, notifications. You don't see them, but they dictate how fast your computer runs, what gets priority, and what crashes first.

Your mind is the same.

Your conscious thoughts are what's visible on the screen. But your subconscious is running dozens of programs in the background, ones you never actively installed. Some are helpful. Others are outdated, slow you down, or constantly glitch.

Good news: Like a computer, you can delete old programs.

Better news: You can install new ones.

I can choose a new script.

How The Inner Critic Gets Programmed

No one is born believing they're not enough. Let's say that again:

You were not born doubting yourself.

That belief came from somewhere. We've mentioned them in previous chapters:

A parent whose tone cut deeper than their words

A teacher who embarrassed you in front of others

A friend whose jokes turned into jabs

A coach who made you feel small or incapable

A society that judged your body, your skin tone, your voice, your ambition, your boundaries

A moment when you needed comfort and instead learned to shrink

Over time, those outside voices become your inner voice. Not because you chose them, but because repetition trains the subconscious.

This is how programming works.

Say it enough times, or hear it enough times, and it becomes law.

Here is your opportunity to stop calling it fate.

The Lenses You Never Chose

By the time we reach adulthood, we carry invisible filters: subconscious lenses that shape how we interpret the world.

Psychologists call these schemas.

Schemas are like tinted glasses you didn't know you were wearing. They color everything: relationships, opportunities, compliments, rejections.

Some common schemas whisper:

- "You'll mess this up."

- "You don't belong here."

- "You're too much."

- "You're not enough."

- "Every one else has it figured out but you."

These messages weren't born from facts. They were born from patterned emotional experiences, and usually painful ones. Schemas can form from abandonment, criticism, neglect, or environments that lacked emotional safety.

For example, if, as a child, you were constantly blamed for things you didn't do, you may develop a defectiveness schema: "Something must be wrong with me."

If you were emotionally abandoned, a rejection schema may whisper: "People always leave me."

Schemas are not the truth.

They're survival stories we internalized.

But here's the key:

Just because a voice lives in your head doesn't mean it deserves authority.

"Schemas aren't facts. They're echoes. And every echo can be quieted."

Your Subconscious In Action: The Horse & Rider

Now let's visualize your inner world.

Imagine your subconscious mind as a horse: powerful, instinctive, fast.

Your conscious mind is the rider: intentional, logical, goal-oriented.

If the rider takes the same trail every day, eventually the horse memorizes it. The rider can drop the reins, and the horse will still go where it's always gone.

That's how habits form.

Now imagine one day the rider says, "Let's take a new trail."

What happens?

The horse resists.

Not because it's bad or broken, but because the old trail is familiar. The rider must be intentional and direct the horse to its destination.

That's your brain.

Every time you try to think a new thought, adopt a new habit, or believe something different about yourself, the horse (your subconscious) pulls back toward the familiar.

But with consistency, the new trail can become the default path.

This is the essence of change.

It's not a one-time push; it's a gentle, repeated redirection.

You're not weak for struggling to change. Your brain is doing what it was designed to do. And you are fully capable of rerouting it.

Exercise Spotlight: Draw Your Future

(Adapted from Patti Dobrowolski's TEDx Talk: Draw Your Future — TEDxRainier)

This exercise is powerful, simple, and science-backed.

Get out a piece of paper. Divide it in half.

1. On the left side, draw where you are now.

   Stick figures welcome.

2. On the right side, draw where you want to be, and use color.

A goal, a vision, a way of being.

3. Draw the bridge in between.

What will get you from here to there?

This isn't art.

It's activation.

Research shows your brain believes images more than words. By drawing your future, you make it real to your subconscious. You start building that new trail for the horse to follow.

So, start drawing.

Start imagining.

Start reprogramming, one image at a time.

I am allowed to want more. I am safe to imagine something different.

What You Resist, Persists

Let's be honest:

Growth is uncomfortable. Healing is messy. And change requires courage.

But what you refuse to look at will rule your life.

When you suppress pain, it burrows deeper. When you name it, it begins to release its grip.

You don't have to carry what you've been carrying. You never did.

Support is out there, and support is for you. Be intentional about finding, accessing, and using it.

You don't have to do this alone.

Rewiring Begins With Awareness

You can't change what you can't see.

But once you see it, even once, you can begin to choose differently.

Not perfectly.

But consciously.

This isn't about "positive vibes only." It's about empowered thinking. About becoming the rider who learns to guide the horse, not through force, but through practice.

The next chapters will give you tools to begin that practice. But for now, start here:

Draw your future.

Name your schemas.

Be gentle with yourself.

You're not reprogramming alone. You're joining a movement of people who are done living by default.

You're starting to live by design.

I hear the voice, but I choose the truth.

I am growing beyond the limits of my past.

I am learning to trust myself again.

CHAPTER FOUR

Schemas, Shadism, and Survival

The Lenses You Never Chose

"You don't see the world as it is. You see it as you were taught to see it."

We all walk around with invisible glasses: lenses that shape how we interpret our experiences, our relationships, and ourselves. Most of us never question these lenses because they feel normal, natural, automatic.

But these lenses are not neutral.

They were shaped by:

- your childhood

- your culture

- your race

- your gender

- your body

- your survival instincts

- the places you grew up

- the voices that raised you

- the wounds that shaped you

This chapter is about the filters you never chose, but have been living through your entire life.

Once you see them, you reclaim the power to adjust the lens.

The Lenses That Live In Your Body

Schemas are the subconscious patterns your brain uses to interpret life.

Think of them like mental shortcuts:

"People can't be trusted."

"I have to be perfect to be accepted."

"If I stand out, I'll be judged."

"I'm responsible for keeping everyone happy."

"My voice doesn't matter."

These are not personality traits. They are survival strategies.

Schemas form from repeated emotional experiences: little moments that stack up over time until they feel like truth. And once a schema is in place, your brain filters the world through it.

You don't see what's happening. You see what you expect.

When Identity Shapes The Lens

Let's talk about something real. Something many self-help books skip because it's uncomfortable.

Shadism: the unspoken hierarchy of skin tones within communities of color. If you grew up as a darker-skinned girl, a Black girl, or a racialized girl, you learned early, often without anyone speaking a word, that the world didn't treat everyone the same.

You felt it: in classrooms, in girlhood friendships, in dating, in compliments withheld, in whose hair was called 'professional,' in who was labeled as having 'attitude' versus being 'assertive,' in which girls got treated softly and which girls were treated harshly even when they needed tenderness.

Shadism is not just societal. It becomes psychological programming.

It teaches you to shrink, to stay quiet, to minimize your emotions, to work twice as hard, to expect rejection, and to accept less: to anticipate judgment before it arrives.

It becomes a schema, a subconscious pattern that says: "Your worth depends on your proximity to their comfort." Not because it's true. But because you learned it before you had the power to challenge it.

Survival Creates Stories

When you're young, and the world treats you differently, you create stories to stay safe:

"I shouldn't speak up."

"If I shine too brightly, I'll be targeted."

"If I show emotion, they'll call me dramatic."

"If I soften, they'll walk all over me."

"If I stand firm, they'll call me angry."

These aren't flaws. They are adaptations. They kept you safe when you were powerless.

But if you're reading this book now, it's because you're no longer powerless. And yet your body, specifically your nervous system, hasn't updated the story.

My Story: Learning To See My Own Lens

Growing up as a young Black girl in Thompson, Manitoba, I learned early that standing out wasn't always safe. I learned to be hyper-aware of tone, expression, body language, and expectations.

I learned to anticipate danger, avoid conflict, shrink my tears, overperform, overachieve, and make everyone comfortable.

Not because that's who I was, but because that's what survival required.

I didn't know it at the time, but my schemas were forming:

"Be small."

"Be agreeable."

"Be useful."

"Be responsible."

"Be strong at all costs."

Those schemas served me, until they didn't. Until they began limiting my joy, my confidence, my voice, and even my destiny.

Sometimes the hardest part of healing is admitting:

What protected you in the past is now hurting you in the present.

Schemas Are Not Just Thoughts: They're Body Responses

Let's bring emotional intelligence into the picture.

Schemas don't just live in your mind. They live in your nervous system.

That's why you can know logically:

"I deserve love."

"I deserve success."

"I deserve rest."

…but your body still reacts with:

Tense shoulders, shallow breathing, a racing heart.

Avoidance, procrastination, people-pleasing.

Perfectionism. Freezing.

Your body learned these pathways long before your mind had language. And the body is always trying to protect you, even if the world you're in now is safe.

Shadism, Racism, And The Critic's Tone

When culture teaches you that your worth is conditional, based on beauty standards, professionalism standards, tone standards, or proximity to whiteness, your inner critic learns those rules.

Your critic becomes:

Policing, controlling, harsh.

Hypervigilant, perfectionistic, and afraid.

This is why you can do everything "right" and still feel "not enough."

Your critic is not your enemy. It's a protector who learned the wrong lessons.

You're not fighting a demon; you're unlearning a lens.

How These Lenses Affect Confidence

When your lens is shaped by survival, it teaches you:

Don't risk.

Don't shine.

Don't be seen.

Don't take up space.

Don't make anyone uncomfortable.

Don't ask for more.

Don't rest.

Don't reveal weakness.

Don't show up fully.

This is not low self-esteem. This is conditioned survival behavior.

You're not lacking confidence. You're carrying generational and experiential programming.

And you can release it.

Reflection Exercise: Identify Your Lens

Write these down:

1. What repeated messages shaped your childhood, spoken or unspoken?

2. What did you learn about worth, beauty, tone, strength, softness, success, failure, anger, ambition, and survival?

3. What did you learn from observing the adults around you?

4. Which of these beliefs still lives in your body?

This is not about blame. It's about clarity.

How To Begin Changing The Lens

You don't fix schemas with force. You change them with:

Awareness

"What lens am I using right now?"

Compassion

"This lens once protected me."

Repetition

"I can choose a new story."

Environment

Surround yourself with people who encourage expansion.

Emotional Intelligence

Understanding when the critic is speaking from fear.

Boundaries

Protecting the healed version of you.

Affirmations

Rewiring at the subconscious level.

I release the stories that were never mine.

I see myself clearly now.

I am worthy without conditions

My past shaped me, but it does not define me.

I choose a lens that honors my truth.

"Your lens is not your identity. It is simply the story your past told your brain."

You Deserve A New Way Of Seeing

Your schemas kept you safe in a world that didn't always honor you.

Your lens helped you survive.

But survival is no longer the assignment.

You are allowed to see yourself, and your life, with softness, truth, clarity, and possibility.

This is the beginning of a new vision.

CHAPTER FIVE

The Comfort Zone & The Lie of Safety

Why Familiar Isn't the Same as Safe

"Familiar does not mean safe. It just means known."

Your comfort zone feels warm. Predictable. Familiar. It feels like a soft blanket on a cold day, until you try to move. Then you realize: it's not a blanket. It's a cage padded with all the things that once protected you.

We don't stay in our comfort zones because life is good there.

We stay because our nervous system has mistaken familiarity for safety.

Let's talk about that.

The Comfort Zone Isn't Comfortable: It's Controlled

Your comfort zone is not defined by joy. It's defined by predictability.

You can feel miserable, unfulfilled, bored, drained, stuck, or unhappy and still stay exactly where you are, because misery is familiar.

Your brain loves what it can predict. Even if it hurts you. So your comfort zone is the place where:

- You know the rules

- You know how to cope

- You know how to perform

- You know how to protect yourself

- You know how people expect you to show up

And that familiarity creates the illusion of safety. But an illusion is still an illusion.

The Lie Of Safety

Your comfort zone whispers:

"Stay quiet."

"Don't take risks."

"Don't stand out."

"Don't rock the boat."

"Don't try something new."

"Don't disappoint anyone."

"Don't show too much emotion."

"Don't stretch."

"Don't leap."

It tells you that staying small protects you. That shrinking keeps you secure. That being agreeable keeps you loved. That never trying prevents disappointment.

But here's the truth:

Your comfort zone doesn't keep you safe. It keeps you the same.

And the same is not what you're called to be.

A Story: When Familiarity Blocks Freedom

I had a client, let's call her Charmaine, who came to see me because she was feeling severely depressed and having suicidal thoughts.

She told me she had experienced bouts of depression throughout her life and had gone from therapist to therapist, never really finding the support that helped her get to the root of the issue.

Over the course of several weeks, Charmaine opened up. She admitted to having made choices in her youth that she was ashamed of, choices she had never truly forgiven herself for. Every time her past came up, a shadow crossed her face. There was no compassion there, only contempt for herself.

Charmaine was also the "strong one" in her circle. The "go-to" person. The one who carried everyone else's burdens. She was deeply empathetic; in fact, I believe she's an empath, someone who feels what others feel as if it were their own pain.

We explored her relationships, and 90% of them were toxic, draining, or one-sided.

As we worked together, light bulbs started to go off for her. She realized how often she had prioritized the needs and emotions of others, never questioning what toll that was taking on her own well-being.

After about six months of progress, we reached the point where we were going to address the deeper wounds, the truths she'd been running from.

And that's when Charmaine pulled away.

She reverted to a familiar pattern: start, then stop.

We had even spoken about this pattern. I told her I'd walk alongside her through the difficult parts. I reassured her that she had the tools, and the strength, to face the truth and move through it.

But the habit won.

The comfort of not going deeper won.

She ghosted therapy: not out of laziness, but out of a nervous system programmed to protect her from pain by avoiding it altogether.

Did you expect this to be a success story?

Charmaine was not ready. Not yet.

She hadn't learned to show herself the same compassion she gave so freely to others. She hadn't made peace with her past. She wasn't ready to leave the version of herself she had always known: the one who endured, carried, survived, and performed.

Does that sound familiar?

Could this be your story?

Because here's the thing: if you are not able to truly love yourself, all parts of you, even the parts you've tried to bury, you will struggle to receive authentic love from anyone else.

You will struggle to create boundaries.

You will struggle to leave unhealthy relationships.

You will struggle to feel worthy, even in spaces where you are valued.

Why The Comfort Zone Feels Like Home

Your comfort zone is built from:

- old wounds
- old roles
- old fears
- old expectations
- old versions of you
- old coping mechanisms
- old stories

- old traumas

- old rules

You didn't consciously choose it; you adapted to it.

As a child, your comfort zone was where survival was predictable. As an adult, your nervous system still chases that predictability, even when it costs you:

- your voice

- your joy

- your potential

- your dreams

- your peace

- your identity

Your comfort zone is not who you are. It's who you had to be.

The Role You Learned To Play

Maybe your comfort zone taught you to be:

- the strong one

- the quiet one

- the fixer

- the overachiever

- the peacemaker

- the invisible one

- the clown

- the "good girl"

- the responsible one

- the one who never needs help

These roles were armor. They protected you. But they are not your identity.

You can thank them for getting you this far.

And then you can release them as you step into who you truly are.

The Biology Of Staying Small

The comfort zone isn't just emotional; it's neurological.

Your brain's number one job is simple:

Keep you alive.

Not thriving.

Not fulfilled.

Not joyful.

Not successful.

Just… alive.

So anything unfamiliar, even if it's good, triggers internal alarms.

Promotion? Scary.

Healthy relationship? Suspicious.

Rest? Uncomfortable.

Joy? Overwhelming.

Boundaries? Dangerous.

Self-trust? Foreign.

Your brain's threat system responds to change the same way it responds to danger. That's why you can want growth with all your heart… and still procrastinate, self-sabotage, or freeze.

You're not weak. Your brain is trying to protect you using outdated information.

Remember Our Computer Analogy?

Let's revisit. Think of yourself like a computer.

You're busy trying to work on the screen, pursuing goals, building relationships, managing life, but there are dozens of programs running in the background that you didn't even open.

Those background programs? They're your subconscious beliefs. Your childhood coping strategies. The rules you never questioned. The roles you were told to play.

Computers run on programs. So do we.

And unless you intentionally identify, update, or close some of those background programs, they'll drain your energy, slow you down, and limit what you're capable of achieving.

Fear Lives At The Edges

A ring of fear surrounds your comfort zone. Every time you get close to the edge:

The critic gets loud.

Your chest tightens.

Your stomach drops.

Your mind catastrophizes.

Your old programming flares.

This is not a sign you're on the wrong path. This is the sign you're on the right one.

Fear doesn't show up to stop you. It shows up to confirm you're expanding.

The Problem Isn't Fear: It's Avoidance

Fear doesn't block growth. Avoiding fear blocks growth.

Your comfort zone tells you that avoiding discomfort is the smart decision. But avoiding discomfort is also how you avoid:

- opportunity

- connection

- healing

- transformation

- abundance

- alignment

Your destiny isn't found in the familiar. It's found in the unknown.

But the unknown is not unsafe; it's just unpracticed.

Reflection: What Has Your Comfort Zone Cost You?

Ask yourself:

1. What have I avoided because it felt "safer" not to try?

2. What roles have I outgrown but still cling to?

3. Whose comfort have I been protecting at the expense of my own growth?

4. What does my inner critic say when I get close to the edge?

Your freedom is hidden inside your answers.

Stepping Out: The First Truth You Need To Know

Leaving your comfort zone won't feel good at first. It will feel:

- shaky

- unfamiliar

- uncertain

- awkward

- vulnerable

- new

But "new" is not danger.

"New" is the beginning of alignment.

And alignment is the beginning of your real life.

I am safe to grow.

I am allowed to change.

Unfamiliar can be good.

I choose courage over comfort.

My future deserves a version of me I have not met yet.

"Comfort is the enemy of growth. Safety is not found in the familiar; it is found in the truth."

Closing: The Invitation To Step Forward

Your comfort zone was built from fear, not freedom. From survival, not self-love. From protection, not purpose.

You don't need to burn it down in one day. You just need one step.

One small moment where you choose:

truth over safety

courage over familiarity

healing over habit

And if you're feeling afraid or overwhelmed, know this: support is out there. Be intentional about finding, accessing, and using it.

This chapter completes Part I: Journey & Awareness.

Next, we move into Part II: Mastery, where you learn how to rewire, rewrite, and rebuild.

"Your comfort zone does not define you. Your choices do."

CHAPTER SIX

Emotional Intelligence

The Skill That Changes Everything

"Emotional intelligence is not who you are. It is a skill you practice."

If Part I of this book helped you understand why you think and feel the way you do, Part II is where you learn how to lead yourself through it.

Because awareness is powerful, but awareness without skill is overwhelming.

That's where Emotional Intelligence (EQ) comes in.

EQ is not about controlling your emotions or pretending everything is fine. It's not about being calm all the time, or positive all the time, or agreeable all the time.

Emotional intelligence is about mastery, not masking.

It is the ability to:

- recognize your emotions

- understand your emotions

- regulate your emotions

- express your emotions

- use your emotions

…without abandoning yourself or hurting others.

If you can learn EQ, you can change your life. And the good news?

You can learn it.

No matter your past.

No matter your personality.

No matter how long the critic has been in charge.

EQ is a skill, not a gift.

The Five Dimensions of EQ (And Why They Matter)

There are many models of emotional intelligence, but the one I use most in coaching, therapy, leadership development, and personal growth includes five core dimensions.

You'll recognize yourself in these.

Self-Perception: How You See Yourself

This is your:

- self-regard

- confidence

- clarity about your strengths

- belief in your abilities

When your self-perception is low, your inner critic becomes the narrator of your life. When your self-perception is strong, you don't silence the critic; you outvote it.

My view of myself matters more than anyone else's.

Self-Expression: How You Communicate Your Inner World

This is:

- being authentic

- being emotionally honest

- expressing needs, boundaries, and feelings

- communicating without apology

Self-expression is not "speaking your mind no matter what." It's speaking your truth with clarity and care, even when your voice shakes.

Most women, especially women who grew up racialized, hyper-responsible, or conditioned for silence, struggle with this dimension.

Self-expression is where we unlearn shrinking.

My voice is safe with me.

Interpersonal Relationships: How You Connect With Others

This includes:

- trust

- empathy

- compassion

- reciprocity

- the ability to give and receive support

Many of us were raised to give endlessly, but taught nothing about receiving. EQ reminds you that a healthy connection requires both.

I deserve relationships where I am supported, not just useful.

Decision-Making: How You Use Emotions to Think Clearly

This is not about being "logical" or "emotional." It's about using both.

People with strong decision-making skills can:

- separate feelings from facts

- consider long-term impact

- avoid impulse reactions

- recognize emotional bias

- trust themselves

When this area is underdeveloped, the inner critic hijacks your choices. EQ helps you regain the driver's seat.

My emotions inform my decisions; they do not control them.

Stress Tolerance: How You Handle Pressure and Uncertainty

This is:

- resilience

- flexibility

- adaptability

- emotional grounding

- the ability not to collapse under stress

Stress tolerance is not the absence of fear. It's the presence of capacity.

You've survived 100% of your hardest days.

This dimension teaches you how to thrive beyond them.

I can handle hard things without abandoning myself.

"Emotional intelligence is not who you are. It is a skill you practice."

The Most Misunderstood Truth: EQ Is Not About Being "Nice"

Too many women are taught that EQ equals pleasantness.

No.

Let me say that louder:

Emotional intelligence is not people-pleasing. Emotional intelligence is personal power.

It is the ability to:

Stay grounded instead of reactive

Choose responses instead of survival patterns

Speak truth instead of shrinking

Hold boundaries instead of resentment

Connect without self-betrayal

Be sensitive without losing strength

Feel deeply without falling apart

EQ is not softness. It's a skill.

Why EQ Matters More Than IQ

IQ helps you do the job.

EQ helps you:

- lead the team

- manage the conflict

- handle the pressure

- build the relationships

- adapt during crisis

- influence outcomes

- stay authentic

- stay aligned

- stay human

Studies consistently show that EQ predicts success more than intelligence, education, or talent alone.

But more importantly? EQ determines the quality of your life.

Your relationships.

Your confidence.

Your boundaries.

Your peace.

Your leadership.

Your healing.

Your self-trust.

Everything you want requires emotional intelligence.

A Story: The Day EQ Changed My Life

Years ago, before AWL Partners, before workshops, before keynotes, before any of the work I now do with confidence, I was still navigating what it meant to lead myself.

And I'll be honest: I didn't always do it well.

I grew up in a household where critique was like oxygen. It wasn't intended to wound; it was meant to build resilience, sharpen you, toughen you up. But to a sensitive child with a tender heart, constant critique didn't feel like guidance. It felt like judgment.

And I internalized it.

Among some friends' parents I got labeled the "Bitch on Wheels." [Note for author: this story also appears in Chapter 2 and is referenced in Chapter 10. Consider consolidating to one chapter and cross-referencing elsewhere.]

That truly hurt to the core.

I was assertive. Direct. Opinionated. But I was also hurting. I had never learned how to separate feedback from shame. So when someone disagreed with me, I'd get defensive. When I got a critique, I'd either argue to the death or smile through clenched teeth while seething inside.

I couldn't take it in because I had no emotional container to hold it. Critique didn't feel like help; it felt like proof that I wasn't good enough.

But then something changed.

A friend and colleague stopped me one day and asked me why I get so defensive when I'm critiqued. She explained that people are trying to help me, not hurt me.

PAUSE

That caring side conversation changed everything.

I started studying emotional intelligence, not as a buzzword, but as a survival skill. I began to unpack my patterns. To ask myself, "Why do I react like this?" To notice the stories I'd been told, and the ones I was still telling myself.

And then I started teaching it.

Funny thing about teaching: it holds a mirror up to your own gaps. I couldn't help others navigate hard feedback if I hadn't done the work myself. So I practiced. And practiced. And practiced.

I stopped avoiding feedback and started translating it. I stopped reacting to my wounds and started responding from my wisdom.

It wasn't overnight. And I still catch myself sometimes.

But over time, I rewired the way I experienced critique. I didn't become perfect. I became whole.

That is emotional intelligence in action.

Not calmness.

Not pleasantness.

Not perfection.

Alignment.

How Your Inner Critic Disrupts EQ

Every dimension of emotional intelligence is affected by the critic:

Self-perception: "You're not enough."

Self-expression: "Stay quiet."

Interpersonal relationships: "Don't be a burden."

Decision-making: "You'll choose wrong."

Stress tolerance: "You can't handle this."

Your critic doesn't want you to think clearly; it wants you to think fearfully. And fearful thinking sabotages emotional intelligence.

This chapter begins the work of separating your critic from your capacity. Because once you do?

You stop reacting to old wounds and start responding from a place of emotional mastery.

Reflection Exercise: Your EQ Snapshot

Take a moment and rate yourself from 1 to 10 on each dimension:

Self-Perception

O O O O O O O O O O
1   10

Self-Expression

O O O O O O O O O O
1   10

Interpersonal Relationships

O O O O O O O O O O
1   10

Decision-Making

O O O O O O O O O O
1   10

Stress Tolerance

O O O O O O O O O O
1   10

Then ask:

- Where do I feel strongest?

- Where do I feel most activated?

- Where do I default to old programming?

- What does my critic say in this dimension?

- What would my emotionally intelligent self say instead?

Awareness creates choice. Choice creates mastery.

I can feel and still choose.

My emotions guide me.

I trust myself.

I lead with emotional intelligence

I am becoming who I am meant to be.

Reminder: You Don't Have To Do This Alone

Emotional intelligence is a personal journey, but it's not a solo one.

Support is out there. Be intentional about finding, accessing, and using it. Therapists. Coaches. Peer groups. Podcasts. Books. Programs. Safe friends. Community.

You don't need to be perfect to be supported. You just need to start.

Closing: This Is Where The Mastery Begins

In Part I, you learned the voice of the critic.

In this chapter, you learned the language of emotional intelligence.

The next chapters show you how to retrain your mind, reprogram your beliefs, and rebuild your self-trust using powerful frameworks designed for real life.

We're moving from understanding to rewiring.

CHAPTER SEVEN

Rewriting Your Script

The P.A.I.D. Method™

"Awareness shows you the script. P.A.I.D.™ helps you rewrite it."

By now, you've learned that your inner critic is not the truth; it's a program.

A subconscious script written years ago. A story built from survival, culture, conditioning, wounds, and repetition.

But here's the beautiful part:

If a story can be learned, it can be unlearned. If a script can be written, it can be rewritten.

This chapter introduces the method I created after two decades of therapy, coaching, emotional intelligence work, and my own healing journey.

It's simple.

It's powerful.

And it works when you work it.

Welcome to the P.A.I.D. Method™:

P = Pattern Recognition

A = Awareness Building

I = Intentional Rewiring

D = Daily Repetition

Let's break it down.

P = Pattern Recognition

You cannot change what you will not name.

Patterns are sneaky. They disguise themselves as personality.

You say:

"I'm just an overthinker."

"I'm just sensitive."

"I'm just indecisive."

"I'm just a perfectionist."

"I'm just the strong one."

But these aren't personality traits. They are patterns of protection.

Before you can change them, you must see them.

Pattern Recognition Questions

- When does my critic speak the loudest?

- What triggers my spirals?

- What do I avoid?

- What do I tolerate even though it hurts me?

- What roles do I slip into when I'm stressed?

- What do I believe about myself when I'm upset, overwhelmed, or tired?

Patterns always reveal two things:

1. What you fear

2. What you've rehearsed

And once you recognize your script, everything shifts.

My patterns are learned. I can learn new ones.

A = Awareness Building

Understanding is the antidote to shame.

Awareness is the moment you say:

"Oh. I know where this comes from."

It's the bridge between your past and your power.

Awareness asks:

- Whose voice am I repeating?

- When did I first learn this belief?

- What was happening in my life when this script was written?

- What was I trying to protect myself from?

When you answer those questions honestly, something profound happens:

The shame loosens.

The pattern softens.

The critic quiets.

The truth emerges.

Because the moment you understand a behavior, you stop blaming yourself for it.

Truth Most People Miss

Your patterns were not signs of weakness. They were signs of survival.

Awareness turns judgment into compassion.

And compassion is what makes change possible.

What I understand, I can transform.

I = Intentional Rewiring

Your brain believes what you repeat.

This is the rewiring stage, the stage where you decide: "I'm choosing a new story." This step is not about lying to yourself or pretending everything is perfect. It's about choosing beliefs that support who you're becoming.

Because subconscious programming changes through:

- repetition

- visualization

- language

- emotional resonance

- practice

How to Rewire a Belief

Identify the old belief:

"I always mess things up."

Find the evidence against it:

(Your brain needs proof. Be as specific as you can be.)

"I've succeeded many times. I learned from my mistakes."

Choose a believable bridge belief:

Not toxic positivity. Not delusion. A bridge:

"I'm learning to trust myself more each day."

Speak it. Write it. Repeat it.

Your subconscious listens to consistency, not intensity.

Why "Believable" Matters

If you jump from "I'm a failure" straight to "I love myself fully," your brain throws the whole thing out.

But if you shift to:

"I'm learning to show up for myself,"

your brain says, "Okay. That's doable."

The rewiring begins.

D = Daily Repetition

This is where transformation happens.

Your critic is loud because it's practiced. Your confidence will become loud because it's practiced, too.

Daily repetition is where new neuropathways form. Where new emotional patterns emerge. Where a new identity takes shape.

Repetition is not glamorous.

It's not dramatic.

It's not Instagrammable.

But it is the difference between trying and changing.

Daily Practice Ideas

morning affirmations

evening journaling

gratitude lists

mirror work

breathing exercises

visualization

5-minute self-check-ins

choosing one brave action a day

saying "no" once a week

celebrating your wins out loud

Your subconscious learns through consistency. The more you repeat your chosen belief, the more natural it becomes.

Small daily actions create massive internal shifts.

Putting It All Together: A Real-Life Example

Let's say your pattern is: "I downplay my accomplishments."

P = Pattern Recognition

You notice you deflect every compliment.

A = Awareness Building

You trace it back to childhood:

You weren't allowed to brag.

You were told humility meant silence.

Your critic learned that visibility is dangerous.

I = Intentional Rewiring

You choose a new belief:

"It is safe for me to be proud of myself."

You practice saying:

"Thank you. I worked hard on that."

D = Daily Repetition

You set a reminder each night to name one thing you're proud of. Over time, your nervous system rewrites the script. Visibility no longer feels dangerous. It feels aligned.

That is the power of the P.A.I.D. Method™.

Reflection Exercise: Your Script Rewrite

Answer these:

1. What is one pattern you want to change?

e.g., overthinking, apologizing, people-pleasing, freezing, and/or perfectionism.

2. What does this pattern protect you from?

Rejection? Criticism? Conflict? Disappointment?

3. Whose voice does this pattern belong to?

Parent? Teacher? Culture? Past version of you?

4. What bridge belief will you practice instead?

Choose something compassionate and believable.

5. What daily action will reinforce it?

Small, simple, repeatable.

You don't need a new life. You need a new script.

And you're writing it right now.

Closing: You Are Not Starting Over. You Are Rewiring Forward.

The P.A.I.D. Method™ isn't about becoming someone new. It's about becoming the person you were always capable of being: despite the programming, despite the fear, despite the shame, despite the shrinking, despite the critic that learned how to keep you safe by keeping you small.

This work isn't erasing your past. It's updating what no longer serves you.

Every time you pause, notice, question, and choose differently, you are teaching your mind a new way to respond to the world. You are interrupting patterns that once ran automatically. You are creating space where there used to be reflex.

That matters.

Your power was never lost. It wasn't taken from you. It wasn't something you failed to develop.

It was buried and layered over by experiences, expectations, and survival strategies that once made sense. And now, with patience and intention, you are excavating it.

Not all at once. Not perfectly.

But one thought, one choice, one moment at a time.

This is not starting over. This is moving forward with awareness, with agency, and with growing trust in yourself.

And that changes everything.

CHAPTER EIGHT

From Self-Doubt to Self-Trust

The T.A.G. Method™

"Self-trust is not built by being fearless. It is built by choosing yourself even when you are afraid."

You can rewrite your thoughts (Chapter 7), but if you don't rebuild trust with yourself, your inner critic will always find a way back in.

Because at the heart of every spiral, every doubt, every freeze response, every moment you shrink, every time you procrastinate, every time you overthink…

…there is one core wound:

Self-distrust.

Not trusting your voice.

Not trusting your judgment.

Not trusting your instincts.

Not trusting your worth.

Not trusting you can handle the outcome.

Not trusting that you are enough.

So let's rebuild that foundation, because everything else rests on it.

Welcome to the T.A.G. Method™, the three-step process I use with clients, leaders, women in my workshops, and in my own life:

T = Tell Yourself the Truth

A = Affirm Your Capacity

G = Give Yourself Proof

From spiraling → solid.

From doubting → deciding.

From fearing → trusting.

Let's go.

T = Tell Yourself the Truth

Self-doubt thrives in stories. Self-trust thrives in truth.

Your critic doesn't lie in obvious ways. Its lies sound like logic:

"You've failed before."

"You don't know what you're doing."

"They won't take you seriously."

"You're too emotional."

"You need more time."

"You're not ready."

The critic presents these statements as facts. But they are not facts. They are fear-based interpretations.

Telling yourself the truth means interrupting the critic's narrative.

Truth Questions

- What is actually happening right now?

- What part of this is fear, not fact?

- What evidence do I have that I'm capable?

- Is this my voice or an old voice?

- What is the real truth beyond the emotion?

Telling yourself the truth doesn't silence the critic completely, but it puts the critic on trial.

And when truth is present, fear loses its power.

I honor myself by choosing the story that supports me.

A = Affirm Your Capacity

Self-trust isn't built by believing you'll never fall. It's built by remembering you know how to rise.

When you doubt yourself, your brain is not doubting your worth; it's doubting your capacity.

Capacity: your ability to navigate uncertainty, handle emotions, adapt, learn, choose, and recover.

You have forgotten your capacity because survival taught you to focus on danger.

Affirming your capacity means reminding your nervous system:

"I've done hard things before. I can do this too."

Capacity Reframes

"I don't know everything," → "But I know how to figure things out."

"This is new," → "But new does not mean dangerous."

"I feel scared," → "But I can feel scared and still move."

"What if I fail?" → "What if I learn?"

Affirmations are not fluffy. They are neural reminders. Every time you affirm your capacity, you interrupt your old fear script.

I trust myself to handle whatever comes.

G = Give Yourself Proof

Action is the cure for doubt. Evidence is the cure for fear.

This is the step most people skip. They try to think their way into self-trust.

But trust is built through behavior, not thoughts.

You didn't lose trust in yourself overnight. It eroded gradually, through:

- broken promises to yourself

- abandoned goals

- ignored boundaries

- staying in situations too long

- choosing others over yourself

- silencing your truth

- shrinking your needs

So trust must be rebuilt the same way:

One consistent action at a time.

This is why the G in T.A.G. stands for Give yourself proof. You need evidence that you can:

- follow through

- speak up

- set boundaries

- keep promises to yourself

- make aligned decisions

- act even when afraid

Proof Builders

Say you'll drink one glass of water → drink the glass of water.

Say you'll make one phone call → make one phone call.

Say you'll rest for 10 minutes → rest for 10 minutes.

Say you'll send the email → send the email.

Small.

Simple.

Specific.

Every completed action becomes a vote:

"I can trust myself."

Every vote weakens the critic. And eventually, self-trust becomes your default.

Every small action is proof of my power.

This Is How You Turn Self-Doubt Into Self-Trust

Let's walk through a real example.

Scenario

You want to speak up in a meeting, but your chest tightens, and your critic screams:

"They're going to judge you."

T = Tell Yourself the Truth

"They may or may not agree. But silence will bother me more than disagreement."

A = Affirm Your Capacity

"I can handle discomfort. I can express myself clearly."

G = Give Yourself Proof

You share one short point.

You breathe.

You survive.

You realize it wasn't dangerous.

That moment becomes evidence.

Repeat that enough, and your critic loses authority.

The Nervous System Side of Self-Trust

Your critic lives in your mind. Your distrust lives in your body.

When you were younger, you learned:

- not to speak

- not to question

- not to shine

- not to disagree

- not to advocate

- not to rest

- not to want more

Your body remembers that.

Self-trust requires teaching your nervous system a new truth:

"I am safe now."

Every time you practice the T.A.G. Method™, you retrain your brain-body connection. You stop reacting from fear and start responding from truth.

The Bridge Between P.A.I.D.™ And T.A.G.™

P.A.I.D.™ rewrites your thoughts.

T.A.G.™ rebuilds your self-trust.

You need both.

Without P.A.I.D.™, you may try to build trust on a foundation of lies. Without T.A.G.™, you may rewrite thoughts without changing your life.

Together, they are a full rewiring system.

Reflection Exercise: Your T.A.G. Map

Choose one area where you doubt yourself: work, relationships, boundaries, speaking up, rest, visibility, saying "no," trying something new.

T = Tell Yourself the Truth:

What is actually true here?

What is the critic exaggerating?

A = Affirm Your Capacity:

What strength, skill, or past success can you remind yourself of?

G = Give Yourself Proof:

What is one small action you can take today to vote for the trusting version of you?

Do not underestimate small actions. They are the bricks of your new identity.

"Self-trust is not built by being fearless. It is built by choosing yourself even when you are afraid."

Closing: Trust Is A Lifestyle, Not A Moment

Self-doubt is loud because it's familiar. Self-trust becomes loud because it's practiced.

The T.A.G. Method™ is not a one-time exercise; it is a new way of relating to yourself.

You are not trying to become perfect.

You are learning to trust your voice, your capacity, your truth, and your power.

This chapter marks a turning point: from healing your past to leading your present.

CHAPTER NINE

Perfectionism, Procrastination, & The Frozen Self

You're Not Avoiding the Task. You're Avoiding the Feeling.

"Perfectionism is fear in high heels. Procrastination is fear in pajamas. Freeze is fear in silence."

People think procrastination means laziness. They think perfectionism means high standards. They think freezing means a lack of discipline.

But the truth is simpler. And deeper.

Perfectionism, procrastination, and freezing all come from the same root: Fear.

- Fear of failing.

- Fear of disappointing others.

- Fear of being judged.

- Fear of being seen.

- Fear of being wrong.

- Fear of the unknown.

- Fear of not being enough.

- Fear of losing control.

These behaviors are not character flaws. They are protection mechanisms born from programming, reinforced by the inner critic, and kept alive by a nervous system that believes discomfort equals danger.

Let's break down each pattern so you can see what's really happening underneath the surface.

Perfectionism: When "Not Good Enough" Becomes A Lifestyle

Perfectionism is not the pursuit of excellence. It is the avoidance of shame.

You learned perfectionism early:

- in families where mistakes were criticized

- in classrooms where you were the "smart one"

- in cultures where girls were expected to be twice as good

- in workplaces where racial bias meant no room for error

- in relationships where love felt conditional

- in communities where being "strong" was the only acceptable option

Perfectionism Taught You That

flaws = rejection

mistakes = danger

rest = weakness

slowing down = slipping

asking for help = incompetence

Your critic reinforces this by whispering:

"You can't mess this up."

"You have to be impressive."

"You need to prove yourself."

"You must get it right before you start."

But perfectionism is not about doing things well. It's about never feeling safe enough to be human.

The Psychology Behind Perfectionism

Perfectionism is an emotional regulation strategy.

When you don't feel in control internally, you try to control everything externally. It's a trauma response dressed up as standard-setting.

And the cost?

Your joy.

Your creativity.

Your voice.

Your peace.

Your authenticity.

Your freedom.

I am allowed to be human, not perfect.

Procrastination: The Illusion Of "Later"

You're not putting it off because you don't care. You're putting it off because you care too much.

Procrastination is not a motivation issue. It's a fear-and-overwhelm issue.

Your brain procrastinates when:

the task feels emotionally risky

the outcome feels uncertain

you fear judgment or failure

you lack clarity about where to start

your nervous system is overwhelmed

your inner critic is loud

the task activates old wounds

The Procrastination Loop

1. You think about the task.

2. Your critic predicts failure.

3. Your nervous system activates fear.

4. You avoid the task to feel safe.

5. Temporary relief reinforces the avoidance.

6. Shame kicks in.

7. The task feels even bigger.

8. Repeat.

Procrastination isn't avoidance of the task; it's avoidance of the emotions connected to the task.

This is why "Just do it!" doesn't work.

You don't need discipline.

You need emotional safety.

I can take one step.

The Frozen Self: When Fight Or Flight Becomes "Fawn Or Freeze"

Freezing is not failure. It is a nervous system stuck in protection mode.

Freezing is the least understood trauma response, yet one of the most common in women who were raised to:

- be responsible

- be strong

- please others

- avoid conflict

- stay small

- stay agreeable

- anticipate danger

- outrun judgment

What Is Fight, Flight, Freeze, Fawn?

These are your body's automatic survival responses to perceived danger.

Fight: Confronting the threat.

Flight: Escaping or avoiding the threat.

Freeze: Becoming immobilized when escape or confrontation feels impossible.

Fawn: People-pleasing or appeasing to reduce threat and gain safety.

When you freeze, your body is saying:

"This feels too big."

"This feels too dangerous."

"This feels too overwhelming."

"I don't know the next step."

"I need a moment to protect myself."

Freezing is not a sign of weakness. It is a sign of overload.

What Freeze Looks Like

- staring at the screen

- scrolling mindlessly

- cleaning instead of working

- feeling blank

- feeling stuck in your head

- wanting to start but not being able to

- feeling tired for no reason

- doing nothing but feeling exhausted

Freeze is not about willpower. It's about your nervous system hitting the brakes.

My freeze response is trying to protect me.

The Shared Root: The Fear Of "Not Enough"

Perfectionism says: "I must be flawless to be enough."

Procrastination says: "I'll wait until I feel enough."

Freeze says: "I'm overwhelmed because I don't feel enough."

These are all symptoms of the same deep wound:

"Who I am is not enough to be safe."

This belief was planted long before adulthood. But it's running your present life like outdated software.

The work now is not to push harder; it's to reprogram the root.

Why These Patterns Feel So Automatic

Your brain loves efficiency. It chooses familiar patterns because they're faster than creating new ones.

If your brain has practiced:

avoiding risk

overthinking

self-criticism

delaying action

staying small

...for 20, 30, 40 years, then of course these patterns feel automatic.

They are automatic.

But automatic does not mean permanent.

The Critic's Role In These Patterns

The critic fuels all three patterns:

Perfectionism:

"You can't start until you're perfect."

Procrastination:

"You're going to fail anyway, so you better wait."

Freeze:

"It's safer to do nothing than to do the wrong thing."

Your critic believes it is protecting you. It's trying to prevent:

- embarrassment

- judgment

- rejection

- disappointment

- emotional pain

But safety based on fear is not safety. It's imprisonment.

Breaking The Cycle: The Emotional Intelligence Approach

1. Name the Pattern

Awareness interrupts autopilot.

2. Regulate Before You Act

A regulated nervous system enables action. Try:

deep breathing

grounding exercises

shaking out your hands

tapping

a 30-second reset

3. Shrink the Task

Your brain can handle a small action. Not a mountain. Break the task into:

one step

then the next

then the next

4. Lower the Stakes

Instead of "This must be perfect," try:

"This must be real."

"This must be done."

"This must be honest."

Not perfect: present.

5. Celebrate Micro-Wins

This builds dopamine, a neurotransmitter associated with motivation, reward, and pleasure. When you celebrate a small success, your brain gets a little dopamine hit, which reinforces the behavior and increases the likelihood that you'll do it again.

Dopamine builds motivation

Motivation builds self-trust

Self-trust weakens the critic

Consistency beats intensity every time.

Real-Life Example: The Spiral Before The Step

A woman in one of my workshops once said:

"Every time I try to start something important, I freeze. I don't know why."

We unpacked it. She wasn't afraid of the task. She was afraid of:

- disappointing someone

- doing it wrong

- looking incompetent

- confirming her critic's voice

Once she named this, we practiced:

30 seconds of grounding

reframing the belief

choosing a single step

celebrating completion

Two weeks later, she emailed me:

"I didn't become more disciplined. I became more honest."

That is the power of emotional intelligence.

Reflection Exercise: Identify Your Pattern

Choose one situation in your life where you tend to perfect, procrastinate, or freeze.

Answer:

1. What emotion am I trying to avoid?

Fear? Shame? Uncertainty? Disappointment?

2. What story is my critic telling?

3. What truth can I tell myself instead?

4. What is one small next step?

5. How will I celebrate completion?

This is mastery.

I am safe to take imperfect action.

One step is enough.

I choose progress over perfection.

I trust myself to begin.

My pace is valid.

self-compassion + small action = momentum

Closing: You Are Not Stuck. You Are Overloaded.

The frozen self is not your identity. It is a moment. A pattern. A nervous system response doing its best to protect you.

When your system is overloaded, pause looks like failure and stillness feels like being stuck. But that isn't what's happening here. Your body and mind have been carrying more than they were meant to hold, and slowing down became a form of survival.

That doesn't make you weak. It makes you human.

And patterns, once understood, can be unlearned. Fear, once recognized, can be rewired. Trust, once interrupted, can be rebuilt.

Momentum, once lost, can be created again: gently, gradually, and on your terms.

You are not behind. You are not broken. You have not missed your moment.

You are emerging, with more awareness, more compassion, and a deeper capacity to move forward than you had before.

And that matters.

CHAPTER TEN

The I Hate Exercise

Transforming Your Triggers

"Anger is a doorway. Walk through it, and you'll find your truth waiting."

The Workshop With A Huge Impact

I went to a workshop once where the facilitator asked us to write down three things that we hated. There were about fifty women in the room, and we all looked at her like she had three heads.

She must've felt the resistance, because she didn't hesitate; she demonstrated the exercise herself.

She took a deep breath… and began to scream.

Sounds odd, right? Now imagine witnessing it firsthand.

She screamed that she hated certain family members for what they did to her as a child. She screamed that she hated some of her business failures. Her voice cracked. Her face turned red, and her words came out like fire.

It was raw.

It was uncomfortable.

It was powerful.

And when she finished, it felt like watching someone be reborn.

To be honest, I thought she had gone mad.

But then she invited each of us to come to the front and scream our list. Not whisper. Not explain. Do not journal privately. Scream.

It felt terrifying and liberating. To say it out loud was like taking a load off our shoulders that we didn't even realize we were carrying.

That experience changed me. It was so impactful that I brought it back to my team, and it's now a signature part of our online program, Slay Your Inner Critic. We call it the "I Hate" Exercise, and it remains one of the most powerful emotional breakthroughs in our work.

Every time we use it, there's hesitation at first. But once people begin, many cry. Others shake. Some laugh. And almost everyone leaves feeling lighter.

Because expressing what you hate is not negative. It is an opportunity to be honest.

And honesty is the root of healing.

What You Hate Reveals What Needs Healing

"Hate" is a strong word. Most women avoid it not because they don't feel it, but because they were never given permission to name it.

You were likely taught:

- to be nice

- to be agreeable

- to be forgiving

- to be understanding

- to give grace

- to keep the peace

- to hold it together

- to take on emotional labor

But here's the truth, no one teaches us:

Hate is a teacher.

Hate is data.

Hate is a mirror.

Hate is a map.

Your hate does not make you a bad person. It makes you an honest one.

And when you learn to explore it safely, you unlock a deeper understanding of your wounds, needs, boundaries, and power.

Why This Exercise Works

You can't heal what you won't acknowledge. And you can't acknowledge what you won't name.

"I hate…" statements drag the truth to the surface. Not so you stay in the emotion, but so you can transform it.

Because under every "I hate…" is a boundary, a need, a truth.

Let me show you:

Example 1

"I hate when people don't listen to me."

I need to feel heard.

I need to feel seen.

I need conversations where my voice matters.

Example 2

"I hate when I second-guess myself."

I need more self-trust.

I need to stop seeking external validation.

I need to believe that my voice is enough.

Example 3

"I hate being taken advantage of."

I need stronger boundaries.

I need to stop betraying myself to make others comfortable.

The hate isn't the problem. The unmet need is.

Why Women Struggle To Name Hate

You may have been conditioned to:

- play small

- be polite

- avoid conflict

- be the bigger person

- swallow your anger

- soften your tone

- take on emotional labor

Because in this world:

Assertive = "Aggressive"

Honest = "Dramatic"

Emotional = "Unstable"

Direct = "Intimidating"

Anger in women has been punished.

But here's the deeper truth: hate is often just unprocessed anger.

And bottled anger doesn't disappear.

It turns into:

- Resentment

- Anxiety

- Depression

- Self-abandonment

- Perfectionism

- People-pleasing

- Disease

"Hate" is not the villain here. Avoidance is.

The "I Hate" List: How to Do It

This exercise can be triggering. Please ensure you have a support person (counselor, friend, or family member) on standby in the event you need to debrief.

Take out a pen and paper. At the top, write:

"I hate…" Then pour.

Do not censor.

Do not explain.

Do not justify.

Do not be nice.

Do not therapize it.

Just write.

For example:

- I hate feeling invisible.

- I hate being dismissed.

- I hate carrying everything alone.

- I hate when people weaponize my kindness.

- I hate how hard I am on myself.

- I hate pretending I'm fine.

- I hate that I shrink to fit in.

- I hate that I don't feel safe to speak.

- I hate feeling like I'm never enough.

Keep going until you feel the exhale. You'll know when you hit your truth. It might feel uncomfortable, but it will also feel honest.

Step Two: Transform It

Now take your list. For each statement, rewrite using one of these prompts:

"Underneath this, I need…"

"This reveals that I value…"

"The boundary this points to is…"

"What this shows me about myself is…"

Examples:

"I hate being taken for granted."

Underneath this, I need reciprocity.

"I hate always being the strong one."

I need softness and support.

"I hate how much I criticize myself."

I need compassion and inner trust.

This is the moment where the magic happens.

Emotion becomes information.

Information becomes boundaries.

Boundaries become healing.

Healing becomes power.

The Emotional Intelligence Behind This Exercise

Anger is a secondary emotion. It exists to signal something deeper:

- Pain

- Fear

- Disappointment

- Abandonment

- Shame

- Exhaustion

- Violation

- Unmet needs

When you name the anger, "I hate…," you create space to meet the truth beneath it.

That's emotional intelligence.

Naming → Regulating → Understanding → Transforming

A Story: The Day Anger Saved Me

Years ago, I was overwhelmed, overworked, and over it.

I was showing up for everyone but myself.

Then, one day, after yet another moment of self-betrayal, something rose inside me.

It wasn't sadness.

It wasn't exhaustion.

It was anger.

The kind of anger that says: "Enough."

I sat down and wrote:

- I hate being invisible.

- I hate pretending I'm okay.

- I hate being the strong one every time.

- I hate it when people assume I can handle everything.

- I hate how little space I leave for myself.

And beneath each one?

A truth.

A need.

A boundary.

A memory. A lesson.

That moment was transformational. It shifted something within me.

It was one of the first times I turned my anger into awareness instead of guilt.

Reflection: Your "I Hate" Transformation

1. Write 10 to 20 "I hate…" statements.

2. Choose the three that hit hardest.

3. For each, ask:

What is the unmet need?

What boundary does this point to?

What story have I been carrying?

What truth am I ready to honor?

4. Choose one small action to honor that truth today.

You are not staying in anger. You are learning from it.

I welcome my anger with compassion.

My emotions bring me insight.

I honor my needs.

My boundaries are loving.

My triggers lead me to clarity.

I feel deeply and choose wisely.

I live from my present truth.

I listen to my truth.

"Hate is not weakness. It is a signal. Listen to it."

"You cannot love yourself fully if you are not honest about what hurts."

"Say the hard thing. Then watch your shoulders drop."

"What you hate reveals what you are ready to heal."

You don't need to hold this alone. Speak it. Release it. Reclaim your space.

Closing: The Emotional Alchemy Of Honesty

This chapter marks a turning point.

You are no longer organizing your life around the comfort of the inner critic. You are no longer minimizing your feelings to stay acceptable, manageable, or agreeable. You are beginning to reclaim your truth: carefully, courageously, and without apology.

The "I Hate" Exercise is not about negativity. It is about emotional honesty.

Honesty about what hurts. Honesty about what you needed and didn't receive. Honesty about what you are no longer willing to tolerate. Honesty about the support you deserve to seek, receive, and actually use.

This kind of honesty can feel unsettling. It can challenge old rules about being "nice," "grateful," or "strong." It can stir guilt or fear, especially if you were taught that naming your discomfort would make things worse.

But honesty is not harm. And silence is not peace.

You are not wrong for feeling deeply. You are not dramatic. You are not too much.

You are learning to feel honestly and intentionally, so your emotions no longer run the show from the shadows. You are turning raw feeling into insight, insight into clarity, and clarity into choice.

That is emotional alchemy.

And this?

This is power.

Not the kind that dominates, but the kind that liberates.

CHAPTER ELEVEN

Thought Records for Real Life

Not Just for Therapy Rooms

"Your thoughts are not facts. They are habits."

You might be asking: what's a thought record? A traditional thought record is a tool used in Cognitive Behavioral Therapy (CBT) that helps you look at a situation, the thoughts it triggers, the feelings associated with those thoughts, and the meaning you've assigned to them. It's been described as a structured journal for your thoughts.

They have been shown to be an extremely powerful tool, and they can sometimes feel clinical and tedious, especially when you're spiraling in the parking lot after a meeting.

But the core idea behind thought records is powerful: when you change the meaning you assign to a moment, you change your emotional experience of it. The problem is not the concept; it's the format.

So, in this chapter, we're going to take the therapeutic tool and translate it into something usable, relatable, quick, and grounded in emotional intelligence. It's designed for busy women, overwhelmed minds, triggered nervous systems, and anyone who doesn't have time to do the traditional "mental paperwork." Let's simplify it and make it yours.

What You Feel Is Real. But What You Think Might Not Be.

Here's the truth:

Your emotions are valid.

Your thoughts are not always accurate.

Thoughts = interpretations.

Emotions = responses to those interpretations.

And your interpretations are shaped by:

past experiences

schemas

fear and trauma

attachment wounds

racialized experiences

childhood conditioning

cultural expectations

your critic's voice

This means your brain often responds to the story it created, not the reality you're in.

Thought records help you interrupt the story.

Why Thought Records Work

Your brain jumps to conclusions, catastrophizes, assumes danger, predicts rejection, fills in gaps with fear, and uses outdated information to interpret new events.

Thought records force your mind to slow down.

They help you:

- identify the automatic thought

- name the emotion

- analyze the evidence

- choose a more grounded interpretation

- respond from truth instead of fear

It's emotional intelligence applied in real time.

The In-The-Moment Version: The 5-Minute Reframe

You won't need a journal, but you will need five clear steps you can do anywhere, which replace the rumination with clarity.

It goes like this:

BREATHE — regulate the nervous system first. Then ask:

1. Trigger

What happened? (Not what you felt.)

This step is about the facts, not your feelings.

> "My boss walked past me without saying hello."

> "My partner didn't text me back for two hours."

> "I saw a comment on social media that bothered me."

> "Someone disagreed with me in a meeting."

This step grounds your brain in what actually happened. Not the meaning. Not the assumptions. Not the emotion. Just the event.

2. Thought

What story did my brain tell?

This is the critic's domain.

"They're mad at me."

"I must've done something wrong."

"I'm not important."

"Everyone thinks I'm incompetent."

"People don't like me."

"This will blow up into something huge."

These are interpretations, not facts. When you identify the story, you remove its power.

3. Emotion

What did that story make me feel?

Remember: emotion follows interpretation.

Your emotion is real.

The trigger is real.

The story might not be.

For example:

Thought: "My boss is mad at me." → Emotion: anxiety.

Thought: "My partner is losing interest." → Emotion: fear or insecurity.

Thought: "They judged me in that meeting." → Emotion: shame.

Naming the emotion helps regulate the nervous system.

When you name it, you tame it.

4. Truth

What's the more accurate or compassionate interpretation?

This is where emotional intelligence comes in.

"Maybe they were stressed."

"Maybe they were preoccupied."

"A delayed text doesn't mean disinterest."

"A disagreement is not a rejection."

"I'm interpreting this through an old wound."

"This situation is not evidence of my worth."

This step is not about toxic positivity. It's about accuracy.

You're shifting from:

fear → fact

reaction → reality

criticism → compassion

This is the heart of the reframe.

5. Action

What do I want to do now that I see the truth?

This step moves you from spiraling to self-leadership.

Your choices might include:

- doing nothing

- taking a breath

- clarifying with someone

- grounding yourself

- responding calmly

- letting it go

- addressing a boundary

- returning to work

- choosing a more confident behavior

Without this step, the reframe stays in your mind. With it, you embody the transformation.

A note: thought records are powerful. Journaling the thought record allows you to spend some time with your thoughts, and that's a good thing. The process described above is for when you don't have time to journal and need to do some quick mental processing.

A Real-Life Example From My Own Journey

Years ago, I delivered a presentation to a roomful of leaders. Afterward, one person walked past me without acknowledging me.

My trigger?

They didn't speak.

My thought?

"I must've done something wrong." "This person didn't like my presentation."

My emotion?

Anxiety, embarrassment, self-doubt.

The truth?

"I have no idea what they were thinking. They might have been distracted, rushing, or processing their own thoughts."

My action?

I took a breath. Grounded myself. Reminded myself of the positive feedback I did receive. And kept it moving.

Later that day, that same person emailed to thank me. They had simply needed to rush out.

The critic was loud. But the truth was louder once I stopped and listened.

Why Thought Records Matter In Everyday Life

Regular use of thought records:

- reduces anxiety and emotional reactivity

- increases self-awareness and self-trust

- creates space between trigger and response

- strengthens your EQ

- helps you communicate more clearly

- helps you make cleaner decisions

- prevents spirals and reduces overthinking

- improves your ability to hold boundaries

- strengthens confidence over time

They transform the split-second moments that shape your inner world. You respond as the future version of yourself, not the frightened one from your past.

The Thought Record Script You Can Use Anywhere

Here is the simple script you can say in your head:

1. What happened?

2. What story did I make up about it?

3. How did that story make me feel?

4. Is that story actually true? What else could be true?

5. Now that I know the truth, what's a wise next step?

Six questions. Life-changing results.

Reflection Exercise: Your 5-Minute Reframe

Choose one situation from this week that activated you. Answer:

Trigger: What happened?

Thought: What story did I tell myself?

Emotion: What emotion did that create?

Truth: What is a more accurate interpretation?

Action: What is one action I want to take now?

This is emotional intelligence in motion.

I question the thoughts that hurt me.

My feelings are valid, and my thoughts are flexible.

I choose interpretations that support my peace.

I respond with clarity, not fear.

Closing: You're Not Rewriting Thoughts. You're Rewriting Identity.

What I've experienced is that many people think mindset work is about correcting "bad thoughts." But that's not it at all. When you analyze, question, and reframe a thought, you're not just changing content in your head. You are changing who you believe you are in relationship to the world.

This shift is identity-level change.

You are teaching your brain a new way of relating to the world. Remember, your brain learns through repetition, not insight. Each time you pause instead of spiraling, you are building a new reflex:

catastrophizing → grounding

assuming the worst → considering possibilities

shrinking → responding

spiraling → leading

This isn't thought work where you fix a thought and you're done. What you are doing is training a new way of being.

This is self-liberation.

You are learning to think in a way that protects your peace rather than sabotages it.

You move from survival identity to agency identity.

CHAPTER TWELVE

Boundaries, Beliefs, and Becoming

Identity Through Intention

"Every time you honor a boundary, you honor the future version of you."

When women think about boundaries, they often think about saying no.

But boundaries are not walls, attitudes, or ultimatums.

Boundaries are identity statements.

They say:

What you value

What you allow

What you refuse

What you need

What you deserve

Who you are becoming

A life without boundaries is a life lived in reaction.

A life with boundaries is a life lived in intention.

And when you combine boundaries with belief work and emotional intelligence? You become a version of yourself you've never experienced.

This chapter is about that becoming.

Boundaries: The Architecture Of Self-Respect

"Boundaries are not about keeping people out. They're about keeping yourself intact."

A boundary is simply a limit that protects your emotional well-being.

It is: what you tolerate, what you don't, what you're available for, what you're unavailable for, what behavior aligns with your truth, what behavior doesn't.

Boundaries are not punishments.

They are clear.

And clarity is kindness, to yourself first, and to others second.

Why Boundaries Are Hard For So Many Women

Many women are conditioned to:

- be accommodating

- be "nice"

- be agreeable

- not cause conflict

- not hurt anyone's feelings

- prioritize others

- self-sacrifice for harmony

- avoid being "difficult"

- accept emotional labor

- be endlessly understanding

And because of that conditioning, boundaries can feel like:

- rejection

- selfishness

- coldness

- conflict

- betrayal

But the truth?

A boundary is you choosing yourself without apology.

The Three Types of Boundaries

1. Physical Boundaries

Your body. Your space. Your time.

"I'm not available after 7 PM."

"I need space to think before I respond."

2. Emotional Boundaries

Your peace. Your emotional labor. Your sensitivity.

"I'm not okay with being spoken to that way."

"I'm not responsible for your reaction."

3. Energetic Boundaries

Your spirit. Your capacity. Your bandwidth.

"I don't attend every crisis."

"I choose rest over guilt."

Each boundary is an act of self-honoring.

Beliefs: The Internal Boundaries

"Beliefs are boundaries you set with your own mind."

Beliefs are stories we've repeated so often that they feel like truth.

Some beliefs empower you:

"I can handle hard things."

"I deserve reciprocity."

"I am worthy of rest."

"My voice matters."

Others sabotage you:

"I'm too much."

"I need permission."

"If I say no, they'll leave."

"I can't upset anyone."

"I don't deserve ease."

"I should be able to handle everything."

Your boundaries are shaped by your beliefs.

If you believe "I must keep everyone happy," your boundaries will always leak.

If you believe "My needs matter," your boundaries strengthen.

This chapter helps you align the two.

The Link Between Boundaries and Self-Worth

You cannot consistently set boundaries from a place of insecurity. You must believe:

you deserve peace

you deserve respect

you deserve reciprocity

you deserve time

you deserve honesty

you deserve safety

you deserve gentleness

you deserve joy

Without self-worth, boundaries feel like negotiations.

With self-worth, boundaries become non-negotiable.

Why the Critic Hates Boundaries

Because boundaries disrupt the critic's script.

The critic wants you to:

- keep the peace and avoid discomfort

- stay small, stay silent

- over-function, over-extend

- avoid conflict

- be pleasing

- be predictable

The critic survives by convincing you that your needs are inconvenient, your voice is disruptive, your emotions are "too much," and your limits make you unlovable.

When you enforce boundaries, the critic panics, because you stop living according to fear.

Boundaries are emotional intelligence in action.

Becoming: Identity Through Boundaries

"The woman you are becoming needs boundaries that the woman you were never had."

Every time you set a boundary, you shift identity.

Your nervous system learns:

"I can speak up."

"I can protect my energy."

"I can disappoint someone and survive."

"I can choose myself without guilt."

"I can honor my needs."

You are not just doing boundaries. You are becoming someone who trusts herself enough to set them.

Identity grows through repeated acts of self-respect.

How to Know a Boundary Is Needed

You will notice that a boundary has been crossed because you will likely feel:

Irritated, drained, resentful, depleted, overwhelmed

Unappreciated, taken for granted, invisible

Anxious, guilty for no reason

Resentment = self-abandonment.

Exhaustion = lack of boundaries.

Anxiety = misalignment.

Guilt = programming.

Your body tells you where boundaries belong long before your mind does.

The Boundary Formula (Simple And Powerful)

There is a formula that comes from nonviolent communication that I've adapted and often teach in keynotes, workshops, therapy, and coaching:

"I feel ___ when ___. Going forward, I need ___."

Straightforward.

Clear.

Respectful.

Strong.

Example:

"I feel overwhelmed when I'm given last-minute tasks. Going forward, I need more notice."

"I feel dismissed when my voice is interrupted. Going forward, I need space to finish my sentences."

"I feel drained when we only talk about your problems. Going forward, I need more balance in our conversations."

Boundaries don't require anger. They require clarity.

What If They Don't Like Your Boundary?

Guess what? They likely will not like your boundary, because they benefitted from you not having them.

Boundaries reveal:

who benefits from your lack of them

who respects you

who only respects your compliance

who values your well-being

and who values your convenience

People don't get upset when you set boundaries. They get upset when your boundaries stop benefiting them.

And that is information, not rejection.

A Story: The Boundary That Changed My Life

There was a moment in my life when I realized I had built a reputation for being "the strong one," "the dependable one," "the one who will always say yes."

And I was drowning under the weight of that identity.

The day I said, "I can't do that, I'm at capacity," my voice shook. Not because the boundary was wrong, but because it was new.

That one sentence rewired something in me.

I felt my nervous system shift from survival to self-respect.

Setting that boundary didn't change the world around me. It changed the world within me.

I will be honest with you though: I was scared. Doing something new is often scary. Don't shy away from that. Run towards it.

Reflection Exercise: Your Boundary + Belief Alignment

Choose one area of your life where you feel stressed or resentful.

Ask yourself:

1. What belief is causing the leak?

I can't let anyone down.

I should be able to handle everything.

Rest is unproductive.

2. What boundary would honor the truth of who I'm becoming?

I don't respond to emails after 7 p.m.

I say no without over-explaining.

I take breaks without earning them first.

I don't take responsibility for other people's emotions.

I ask for help instead of pushing through.

3. What small action can I take this week to protect that boundary?

Block my lunch break in my calendar.

Pause before saying yes and ask for time to decide.

Send one honest message instead of avoiding the conversation.

Log off at my agreed-upon time one day this week.

Delegate one task I usually hoard.

Cancel or reschedule one nonessential commitment.

4. What will I tell myself when guilt shows up? Because guilt will show up: that's conditioning, not truth.

Guilt doesn't mean I'm doing something wrong.

Discomfort is not danger.

This boundary is protecting my future self.

I'm allowed to change the rules that hurt me.

Saying no here allows me to say yes where it matters.

Rest and limits make me more effective, not less.

My boundaries protect my peace.

My needs matter as much as anyone else's.

I release the guilt around honoring myself.

I choose the woman I am becoming.

Self-respect is my new normal.

Every boundary is a declaration: I choose myself.

Closing: The End Of Mastery, The Beginning Of Momentum

You've learned how to see your patterns with honesty rather than judgment. You've learned how to understand your inner critic instead of being driven by it. You've learned how to rewire your mind, build self-trust, and take imperfect action when waiting for certainty wasn't an option. You've learned how to honor your needs, set boundaries, and protect your peace.

That is not small work.

This chapter completes Part II: Mastery, where
you learned the tools to transform from the
inside out.

This work you've done here is demanding. It can be exhausting. It can be unsettling. It can ask you to loosen your grip on versions of yourself that once kept you safe.

If you've felt stretched or tired at times, that doesn't mean you're doing it wrong. It means you're doing it honestly.

What you've built in this section is not perfection: it is capacity.

The capacity to pause instead of react. To choose instead of default. To stay present with yourself when it would have been easier to push through or shut down.

That is mastery.

And now, something shifts. You are not ending a phase; you are entering one.

You're ready for Part III: Momentum, where we explore fear, forgiveness, energy, alignment, and what it means to live the J.A.M. Effect in everyday life.

This is where the work becomes embodied: less effortful, more instinctive, more you.

Change is coming, not because you're forcing it, but because you've built the strength to hold it.

You are growing.

You are steadier.

You trust yourself more than you did before.

Let's keep going.

CHAPTER THIRTEEN

Fear (Part 1)

How It Traps You

"Fear isn't the enemy. The lie fear tells you is."

If you're reading this chapter, it means you've done the inner work.

You've faced your critic.

You've explored your patterns.

You've rebuilt trust.

You've set boundaries.

You've rewritten your script.

Now we shift into the thing that stops even the strongest, most capable, most self-aware women:

Fear.

Not the kind of fear that keeps you safe from actual danger.

The kind of fear that keeps you stuck in emotional danger:

fear of judgment

fear of failure

fear of being seen

fear of being wrong

fear of rejection

fear of disappointing others

fear of losing control

fear of looking foolish

fear of success

fear of the unknown

This chapter is about how fear traps you quietly, subtly, intelligently.

Fear Exists For One Purpose: Protection

Fear's job is simple:

Keep you alive.

Not thriving.

Not fulfilled.

Not joyful.

Not aligned.

Alive.

The problem is that your brain doesn't know the difference between a real threat, an emotional threat, a predicted threat, or a remembered threat. So it reacts to all of them as if they are the same.

Your fear system is ancient.

Your life is modern.

And the mismatch can create chaos.

When Fear Gets Mistaken For Wisdom

Here's the tricky part:

Fear doesn't sound like panic. It sounds like logic.

Fear whispers things like:

"This isn't the right time."

"Maybe next month."

"What if you fail?"

"What will people say?"

"Don't rock the boat."

"You're not ready yet."

"Don't make a scene."

"Stay where it's predictable."

Fear disguises itself as:

caution

responsibility

planning

maturity

wisdom

But the real translation is:

"I don't feel safe expanding."

Fear doesn't stop you from doing the thing.

Fear stops you from becoming the version of you who could do the thing.

Fear Vs. Danger: Your Body Doesn't Know The Difference

You can be sitting on your couch, completely safe, and still feel:

tight chest

racing heartbeat

sweaty hands

shallow breathing

brain fog

urge to hide

urge to delay

urge to quit

Why? Because your brain has coded something as a threat, even though your body isn't in danger.

Your boss frowns.

Your partner sounds irritated.

Your friend doesn't text back.

You speak up in a meeting.

You launch something new.

You set a boundary.

You say "no."

You say "yes."

You try something unfamiliar.

Your brain pulls the alarm… just in case.

Fear isn't signaling danger. It's signaling uncertainty.

And your nervous system has learned to fear uncertainty as if it were death.

Fear's Favorite Strategy: The Loop

Fear doesn't need to stop you loudly. It stops you quietly.

It does this through the Fear Loop:

1. Trigger

Something activates old programming.

2. Story

Your critic creates a catastrophic interpretation.

3. Nervous System Response

Your body reacts as if something bad is happening.

4. Avoidance

You delay, hide, freeze, or doubt yourself.

5. Temporary Relief

Avoidance feels good, so your brain reinforces the pattern.

6. Reinforced Fear

Your mind now associates action with danger.

Then the cycle repeats.

Fear isn't powerful.

Repetition is.

The Three Ways Fear Traps You

Fear traps you through three psychological mechanisms:

1. Fear Shrinks Your Vision

When fear is active, you cannot dream. You cannot imagine possibilities. You cannot see your future clearly.

Fear creates tunnel vision.

It reduces your focus to risk, danger, and worst-case scenarios.

You start planning your life around what you're scared of, instead of what you're becoming.

This is how potential dies quietly.

2. Fear Magnifies the Consequences

Fear exaggerates everything.

A simple conversation becomes a confrontation.

A small mistake becomes a disaster.

A new project becomes a threat.

A vulnerable moment becomes humiliation.

A boundary becomes abandonment.

Fear turns the volume up on imaginary outcomes and makes them feel inevitable. It isn't telling you the truth; it's projecting your past.

3. Fear Distracts You With "Safety Work"

Safety work is fear's favorite trick.

Instead of taking the real step, you:

overthink

over-plan

over-prepare

over-analyze

re-read, re-draft

ask more opinions, gather more information

clean your house

scroll for inspiration

stay "productive"

…but never actually move.

It feels like progress, but it's just avoidance wearing a blazer.

A Story: The Fear Of Expansion

There was a chapter in my life when everything was expanding: my work, my voice, my opportunities.

But inside, I was terrified.

I was afraid to be judged.

Afraid to be seen.

Afraid to speak boldly.

Afraid to lead loudly.

Afraid to stand in the fullness of who I was becoming.

I worried:

"What if I can't handle it?"

"What if people tear me apart?"

"What if I'm not enough?"

Fear had convinced me that success was dangerous. Not because it was, but because being visible felt unsafe in my past.

Fear wasn't protecting me from the future. It was protecting me from a memory.

That's how fear traps us.

Fear Doesn't Want To Stop You. Fear Wants To Keep You The Same.

Fear is not evil. Fear is loyal.

It wants to protect the version of you that survived childhood trauma, racialized experiences, scarcity, pressure, shadism, criticism, abandonment, being underestimated, being silenced, being overlooked.

Fear remembers who you had to be.

It doesn't yet understand who you are becoming.

This is why you feel pulled in two directions:

Your soul is calling you forward.

Your fear is pulling you back.

This tension is not a flaw. It is a sign of becoming.

Reflection Exercise: Your Fear Map

When you start to feel fearful, answer these questions honestly:

1. What am I actually afraid will happen?

   Name the specific fear.

2. Where did I learn that this was dangerous?

   Childhood? Culture? Past relationships? Work?

3. Is this fear based on a memory, not the present moment?

4. What does fear think it is protecting me from?

   Rejection? Shame? Embarrassment? Abandonment?

5. What part of me is ready to grow beyond this?

Let your truth speak.

My fear is information, not instruction.

I can feel fear without following it.

I honor the girl who needed fear to feel safe.

The woman I am becoming leads anyway.

"Fear is not a stop sign. It is a story your past is telling your future."

Closing: This Is Only Part One

This chapter has one purpose: to show you that fear is not the enemy. The unconscious way we relate to fear is.

Fear is not a flaw in your system. It is a survival response designed to protect you.

Fear carries data.

It offers information.

It lets you know when something feels uncertain, unfamiliar, or potentially risky.

And that matters.

We don't want to silence fear or override it. We want to listen to it without letting it take the wheel.

Because when fear goes unquestioned, it becomes a trap. It keeps us shrinking, delaying, and waiting for certainty that never comes. It convinces us that safety lives on the other side of perfection.

In Chapter 14, we begin to shift this relationship. We move from fear as the trap, to fear as the teacher, to fear as the doorway you walk through.

Fear doesn't disappear when you grow. What changes is how you respond to it.

There comes a moment, often quiet and unglamorous, when you realize that waiting for fear to leave is no longer an option. Not if you want to live fully. Not if you want to honor your potential.

As Coach Shiley on our team so perfectly says:

"Just do it scared."

Not recklessly.

Not without awareness.

But with discernment, support, and self-trust.

Fear can walk with you. It just doesn't get to decide for you.

This is only part one. And you are just getting started.

CHAPTER FOURTEEN

Fear (Part 2)

How You Break Through

"Courage is not the absence of fear. Courage is the decision to move anyway."

Fear will always exist. That's not the problem.

The problem is the relationship you've had with fear: a relationship shaped by childhood, survival, identity, racialized experiences, and past wounds.

Fear used to be the authority in your life. It used to be the voice you obeyed, the feeling you followed, the warning you trusted.

But now?

Now you have emotional intelligence.

Now you have awareness.

Now you have self-trust.

Now you have tools.

Now, you get to decide who leads.

Fear can ride in the car, but it no longer gets to drive.

This chapter is about reclaiming your steering wheel.

Fear Breakthrough Principle #1: Feel the Fear. Don't Fight It.

You've been taught that the goal is to "get rid of fear." But trying to eliminate fear creates:

shame ("Why am I still scared?")

self-judgment ("I should be over this")

pressure ("I need to be fearless")

emotional suppression ("Just push it down")

Here's the truth your nervous system already knows:

You cannot heal what you are trying to outrun.

The solution is not to fight fear. The solution is to feel fear without being controlled by it.

Fear is a wave. Let it pass through you, not dictate to you.

Try saying:

"I feel fear, and I am still safe."

"I feel fear, and I can still choose."

"I feel fear, and I can still take one step."

This is emotional maturity.

This is self-leadership.

Fear Breakthrough Principle #2: Name the Fear Out Loud

Fear thrives in silence. It grows in the dark. Naming it pulls it into the light.

"I'm afraid of failing."

"I'm afraid of being judged."

"I'm afraid of being seen."

"I'm afraid of being rejected."

"I'm afraid of making the wrong decision."

"I'm afraid of success because success means visibility."

When you name it, the fear loses up to 50% of its power instantly. Labeling fear activates the prefrontal cortex, where the rational brain resides, and reduces amygdala activity.

Naming fear regulates fear.

You can't break through what you won't acknowledge.

Fear Breakthrough Principle #3: Separate Fear From Facts

Fear always feels like truth. That's what makes it convincing.

Fear says:

"They'll think you're foolish."

"They won't support you:"

"You're not ready."

"You can't handle that."

"If you speak up, something bad will happen."

But emotional intelligence asks: Is this fear based on my present reality, or a past experience my body still remembers?

You break through fear by fact-checking it.

Ask:

What is actually happening?

What evidence do I have?

What else could be true?

Is this my fear or an old version of me?

Fear narrows your vision.

Facts expand it.

Fear Breakthrough Principle #4: Shrink the Step

Fear overwhelms you because it makes everything feel huge.

Starting a business becomes "I need to succeed immediately."

Having a conversation becomes "This will destroy everything."

Saying no becomes "They'll be angry."

Applying for a job becomes "What if I embarrass myself?"

Your critic zooms out to the biggest possible consequence. Your job is to zoom in.

Shrink the step until your nervous system can tolerate it.

Instead of: "I have to finish the whole thing."

Try: "I will start for five minutes."

Instead of: "I need to be confident."

Try: "I will speak one sentence."

Instead of: "I must know the whole plan."

Try: "I will take the next right step."

Fear decreases when tasks become manageable.

Fear Breakthrough Principle #5: Choose Curiosity Over Catastrophe

Fear asks: "What if something bad happens?"

Curiosity asks:

"What if this works?"

"What if I enjoy this?"

"What if I grow from this?"

"What if I surprise myself?"

"What if I can handle more than I think?"

"What if this is the beginning of something beautiful?"

Fear imagines failure.

Curiosity imagines possibilities.

The shift is subtle but life-changing.

Fear Breakthrough Principle #6: Create Safety From the Inside

Fear is not just mental: it's biological.

When your body feels unsafe, your brain stops you from moving forward. You cannot break through fear with logic alone. You must work with your nervous system.

Try:

deep belly breathing

box breathing

grounding through your feet

self-hugging (activates the vagus nerve)

progressive muscle relaxation

saying "I am safe" while breathing

placing your hand on your chest

These techniques tell your body:

"We are not in danger."

And when your body believes that, your mind becomes free.

Fear Breakthrough Principle #7: Let Your Future Self Lead

When fear tries to stop you, ask: "What would the future version of me do?"

The confident you.

The healed you.

The aligned you.

The emotionally intelligent you.

The woman who trusts herself.

The woman who knows her worth.

The woman who takes up space without apology.

Let her make the decision.

Let her choose the next step.

Let her lead your momentum.

She already exists. She is waiting for you to catch up.

A Story: Fear As A Doorway

As AWL Partners grew, I received invitations to speak, lead, and create on larger stages.

But every new opportunity made my heart race.

I was afraid of being judged, being misunderstood, being criticized, not being "perfect enough," being too much, not being enough. Messages generated from past experiences.

But each time, I asked myself:

"What would the woman I am becoming do?"

And every time, she chose expansion.

Fear wasn't eliminated. It was overridden by truth.

Fear became a doorway, not a wall.

Reflection Exercise: Your Fear Breakthrough Blueprint

Choose an area where fear is holding you back.

Answer:

1. What exactly am I afraid will happen?

Be specific.

2. Where did I learn that this was dangerous?

3. What is a smaller step I can take?

4. What might be possible if I chose curiosity?

5. What would my future self do right now?

Write the answer.

Then take the smallest possible step.

Momentum is built in micro-movements.

Example Scenario: Speaking Up in a Meeting

1. What exactly am I afraid will happen?

"I'm afraid I'll say something wrong and people will think I'm incompetent."

2. Where did I learn that this was dangerous?

"I learned early on that being visible often led to criticism or dismissal."

3. What is a smaller step I can take?

"I can share one prepared point instead of staying silent."

4. What might be possible if I chose curiosity?

"I might learn that my voice is welcomed more often than I expect."

5. What would my future self do right now?

"My future self would speak once, even if her voice shakes."

Then take the smallest possible step. Share the point.

I can feel fear and still move.

Fear is a signal, not a stop sign.

I am safe to expand.

My future is louder than my fear.

The woman I'm becoming leads me forward.

"Fear doesn't leave. But it loses power when you stop
letting it lead."

Closing: You Are Stronger Than The Story Fear Tells

Fear is not a flaw. It is a signal. It is a memory. It is a protective instinct shaped by moments when safety mattered.

And if fear has been loud for you here, that makes sense. You have been stretching beyond what once felt familiar. You have been asking more of yourself. You have been standing closer to your truth.

But fear is not your destiny.

This chapter marks your shift into active momentum: the place where tools turn into action, insight turns into identity, and fear is no longer something you avoid, but something you learn to move with.

Fear doesn't disappear at this stage. What changes is your relationship to it.

You no longer confuse fear with danger.

You no longer let it decide what you are capable of.

You no longer wait for it to leave before you move.

You are ready for what comes next.

Forgiveness. A deeper clearing. A deeper release. A deeper liberation.

Not because fear is gone, but because you are stronger than the story it tells.

CHAPTER FIFTEEN

Forgiveness (Part 1)

The Wound Beneath the Critic

"You cannot forgive what you have not felt."

Forgiveness is one of the most misunderstood parts of healing. People talk about it as if it's a single moment, like flipping a switch or rising above your feelings.

But forgiveness is not a performance.

It's not forced maturity.

It's not pretending you're okay.

Forgiveness is a process, and only you get to decide the pace.

Most women were taught to:

"Let it go."

"Move on."

"Be the bigger person."

"Just forgive."

"Don't hold grudges."

"Keep the peace."

…but no one taught you how to honor the hurt first. And without honoring the wound, forgiveness becomes emotional bypassing, not emotional healing.

This chapter is not about telling you to forgive. It's about helping you understand the wound that forgiveness will eventually touch.

Why Forgiveness Feels So Hard

For some, forgiveness may feel hard because they may think that forgiveness means:

reconciling

excusing

forgetting

minimizing

allowing access

invalidating your pain

restoring trust too quickly

erasing the impact of someone's behavior

But forgiveness is none of those things on its own.

Forgiveness does not mean:

"It didn't happen."

"It didn't hurt."

"It wasn't wrong."

"It's okay now."

"I should be over it."

Forgiveness is:

"I release the emotional contract that keeps this wound alive in me."

Not for them.

For you.

But before release comes recognition.

The Wound Underneath: Emotional Injuries We Carry

At the center of every deep hurt is a core emotional injury.

Usually one or more of these:

Abandonment

Betrayal

Rejection

Invisibility

Dismissal

Neglect

Disrespect

Shame

Broken trust

Deception

Unmet needs

Unheard feelings

These injuries are not just emotional: they are biological. Your nervous system remembers moments when:

You were not protected.

You were not prioritized.

You were unheard, unseen, or unheld.

Someone's choices harmed you.

Your boundaries were violated.

Your voice was ignored.

Your needs were minimized.

Your innocence was disrupted.

Your identity was questioned.

Forgiveness feels impossible when the wound is still bleeding.

Healing must come first.

The Wound Beneath Your Inner Critic

Your critic didn't appear out of nowhere. It was born the day you realized you couldn't rely on:

the adults around you

the people who were supposed to care for you

the systems meant to protect you

the friends who should have stood with you

the partners who promised safety

the communities that didn't nurture you

Your critic is a shield that formed to protect the wound underneath. But the wound still exists: quiet, buried, tender.

Forgiveness work requires that we go beneath the shield and tell the truth about what hurt.

Forgiveness Requires Grief

Grief is not just about death.

It is about:

lost childhoods

lost innocence

lost trust

lost dreams

lost protection

lost opportunities

lost versions of people

lost versions of yourself

You cannot move forward when you are still grieving backward.

Forgiveness requires emotional honesty, and honesty requires grief.

Let yourself feel what you were not allowed to feel at the time.

You Don't Have To Rush Forgiveness

Forgiveness cannot be forced.

You cannot:

pray your way past the wound

meditate your way past the wound

journal your way past the wound

rationalize your way past the wound

affirm your way past the wound

"positive think" your way past the wound

Forgiveness arrives when the wound is ready.

This is why the pressure to forgive quickly is harmful: it invalidates your healing process.

Your timeline is sacred.

Who You Need To Forgive First

Yourself.

Not because you did anything wrong. But because you may still carry:

shame for staying too long

guilt for not knowing better

embarrassment for shrinking

regret for being silent

self-blame for someone else's behavior

resentment toward your past self

anger for ignoring your needs

confusion about why you tolerated things

Forgiveness begins with compassion toward the version of you who didn't have the tools you have now.

She was doing her best with what she had.

She survived so you could heal.

You honor her by softening, not punishing.

A Story: The Forgiveness That Took Years

There was a time in my life when I made a choice I never imagined I would. I had an affair while I was married.

I don't share this to justify it. I don't share it to vilify anyone else. And I certainly don't share it to elicit sympathy or defend my actions.

What led up to that decision is not mine alone to tell.

But what followed? That part is mine.

It shattered something inside of me.

Not because I got caught. Not because others were hurt, though they were. But because it violated my own values.

The guilt felt bone-deep.

The shame? Unrelenting.

I became the judge, jury, and executioner of my own worth.

If anyone knew, I believed, they would hate me. If my family found out, I'd lose their love. If my friends discovered the truth, they would surely walk away.

Some of that fear came true.

But what surprised me more was what came instead:

People who saw my humanity.

People who didn't excuse the choice, but also didn't let it define me.

People who said, "You are not the worst thing you've ever done."

Their love did what shame never could: it helped me rebuild.

But it took years.

Years to sift through the rubble of my own self-image.

Years to stop punishing myself in quiet, hidden ways.

Years to believe that I could be both someone who had made a harmful choice and someone capable of deep healing, deep love, and profound change.

I still hear echoes of that critic sometimes. She shows up when I feel unworthy. When I doubt I deserve softness. When I brace for people to leave.

But I've learned to meet her with something new:

Not justification.

Not denial.

Compassion.

In one of the coaching programs I took, they said:

"Nothing is good or bad: it just is. Everything happens for our good."

That can feel like a hard truth when you've been through things that cracked you open. But it also means this:

You are still here.

Maybe bruised. But resilient.

This story isn't about seeking forgiveness from others. It's about the decade-long process of forgiving myself. Not by forgetting, but by remembering with gentleness. Not by excusing, but by owning, learning, and growing.

Because that version of me who made that choice? She was hurting. She was lost. She was trying to escape a pain she didn't know how to name.

And now, I honor her: not with shame, but with truth, compassion, and accountability.

That's how real forgiveness begins.

Not for a moment.

As a slow, steady act of love.

Reflection Prompt: What Truth Are You Still Carrying?

Take a quiet moment with yourself and ask:

1. What is the one mistake, choice, or season of my life that I still punish myself for?

2. What did that version of me need that she never received?

3. What would compassion say to her now, not judgment, not justification, just compassion?

4. If I softened even slightly toward that version of me, what might begin to heal?

5. What belief about myself was born from that moment, and is it still serving me today?

Write your answers without filtering.

Forgiveness begins with truth. Truth starts with tenderness.

**I release the shame of who I was, and I honor
the wisdom of who I am becoming.**

This is not denial. This is dignity. This is reclaiming the self your critic convinced you to fear.

"Self-forgiveness is not letting yourself off the hook; it is freeing yourself from the noose of your own shame."

Forgiveness Is Not For The Other Person

It's for the Version of You Still Carrying the Pain.

That version of you:

still jumps when someone raises their voice

still over-explains when misunderstood

still freezes in conflict

still tightens when someone disappoints you

still tries too hard to be enough

still doesn't trust easily

still carries guilt that isn't hers

Forgiveness releases her.

Forgiveness says: "You no longer have to carry this."

Forgiveness turns emotional weight into wisdom.

Reflection Exercise: The Wound Beneath Your Forgiveness

Choose one relationship or situation where forgiveness feels hard.

Ask yourself:

1. What was the real wound beneath the hurt?

   Abandonment, betrayal, dismissal, disrespect?

2. What emotion have I been avoiding?

   Anger? Sadness? Grief? Disappointment?

3. What did I need at the time that I didn't receive?

   "I needed reassurance that I mattered."

   "I needed someone to take my feelings seriously."

   "I needed protection or advocacy."

   "I needed honesty instead of silence."

   "I needed to feel chosen, not tolerated."

4. How did the wound shape my inner critic or my patterns?

"It taught my critic to tell me not to ask for too much."

"It trained me to over-function so I wouldn't be abandoned again."

"It made me stay quiet to avoid conflict."

"It taught me to expect disappointment and brace for it."

"It made me self-blame instead of risk being hurt again."

5. What part of me is still holding the memory?

"The younger version of me who didn't feel protected."

"The part of me that learned to stay alert."

"The version of me that learned to be small."

"The part of me that still expects loss."

"The part of me that learned to survive quietly."

This is the beginning of the release.

I honor the truth of how I was hurt.

My feelings are valid.

Healing takes time, and I am worthy of that time.

I soften toward the version of me who survived.

Forgiveness begins with compassion, not pressure.

"Forgiveness is not letting someone off the hook. It is letting yourself off the hook of carrying the wound."

Closing: This Is Not The End. This Is The Opening.

If this chapter stirred something tender, if it brought up memories, emotions, or sensations that surprised you or hurt more than you expected, please pause here.

That response makes sense.

This chapter is about acknowledgement, not closure. It's about looking at the wound with clarity and compassion: not rushing the process, not spiritualizing the pain, and not bypassing the truth of what was experienced.

This kind of work can be heavy. It can unearth feelings that were buried for a reason, because at the time, you did what you needed to do to survive. If you're feeling raw, emotional, tired, or unsettled, that doesn't mean you're doing this wrong. It means you're doing it honestly.

This is a good moment to take care of yourself.

You might choose to put the book down for now. Take a few slow breaths. Go for a walk. Drink some water. Reach out to a trusted friend, family member, or counselor and let yourself be supported.

You don't have to carry this alone.

What you've done here takes courage. You've been willing to look, to name, and to feel, and that matters. You've come this far, and that says something important about you: you are capable of continuing, at your own pace, in your own way.

This chapter prepares the ground for real, embodied forgiveness: not the kind that rushes or minimizes, but the kind that gently frees your nervous system, your mind, your heart, and your future.

In Chapter 16, we move from wound to release, from pain to peace, from surviving to choosing, from carrying to freeing.

This is not the end. It's the opening.

Take the time you need, and when you're ready, we'll keep going.

CHAPTER SIXTEEN

Forgiveness (Part 2)

Freedom Through Release

"Forgiveness is not something you force. It's something you grow into."

If Part 1 was about the wound, this part is about the release.

Not the kind of release people talk about casually, the "just let it go," the "you should forgive," the "be the bigger person."

This is the kind of release that feels like:

unclenching

exhaling

loosening your grip on the past

reclaiming your present

choosing your peace

trusting yourself again

opening your heart to possibility

letting the injury become wisdom

This is forgiveness as liberation, not obligation.

Let's begin.

Forgiveness Is A Gift You Give To Your Future Self

People say that forgiveness sets the other person free. But the truth?

Forgiveness sets YOU free.

Free from:

- the mental loops

- the emotional weight

- the resentment

- the "what-ifs"

- the replaying

- the longing for accountability

- the expectation of repair

- the grip of the memory

- the heaviness in your chest

Forgiveness is not about minimizing the harm. It's about minimizing the hold that harm has on your life.

Forgiveness Is A Nervous System Shift

Most people don't realize this:

Forgiveness isn't primarily a cognitive decision. It's a physiological one.

The moment you forgive, truly forgive, your body releases tension you didn't even know you were carrying.

Your breath deepens.

Your shoulders soften.

Your chest expands.

Your stomach unclenches.

Your mind quiets.

Your sleep improves.

Your energy returns.

Why? Because holding resentment keeps your nervous system in a state of hypervigilance: waiting for an apology, waiting for justice, waiting for acknowledgment, waiting for validation.

Forgiveness releases you from waiting.

It allows your body to come home and truly experience peace.

Forgiveness Does Not Require

- reconnection

- conversation

- reconciliation

- trust

- restoring the relationship

- telling them they were right

- pretending it didn't hurt

- seeing them again

- minimizing your experience

Forgiveness is an internal shift.

The other person never needs to know.

What Forgiveness Does Require

1. Acknowledging the harm

You cannot release what you refuse to name.

2. Feeling the emotion

Not forever, just honestly.

3. Accepting that the past cannot change

This is often the hardest part. You grieve the version of the story you wish you'd lived.

4. Reclaiming your power

You stop waiting for the wound to be undone.

5. Choosing peace over resentment

Not because they deserve it, but because you deserve rest.

Forgiveness is an act of self-respect.

The Truth About Accountability

Many people don't want forgiveness. They want justice.

They want:

- the apology

- the explanation

- the change

- the accountability

- the ownership

- the amends

And when they don't get these things, forgiveness feels impossible.

But here is the liberating truth:

Accountability is external.

Forgiveness is internal.

You cannot control the external. You can choose the internal: you can choose your peace.

Letting Go Does Not Mean Letting In

A crucial distinction:

You can forgive someone and never let them back in your life.

Re-entry is not a requirement.

Access is not automatic.

Forgiveness is release.

Boundaries are protection.

You can have both.

Forgiveness and Identity: Becoming the Next Version of You

When you forgive, you don't just release the pain. You release the version of yourself who carried it.

You release:

- the hypervigilant you

- the fearful you

- the resentful you

- the over-explaining you

- the self-blaming you

- the people-pleasing you

- the mistrustful you

- the shrinking you

Forgiveness is not weakness.

Forgiveness is transformation.

It creates space for:

- softness

- trust

- intuition

- joy

- creativity

- clarity

- alignment

- healthy relationships

- emotional safety

Forgiveness isn't about excusing the past. It's about opening the door to your future.

A Story: Little By Little, Lighter And Lighter

One of my clients, Samira, came to me with a lifetime of tension wrapped tightly around her relationship with her mother.

She described her mother as manipulative, self-serving, and emotionally absent during her most vulnerable years. There were moments when Samira needed comfort but received criticism instead. Times when she needed protection but was told to "toughen up." Love felt conditional. Kindness felt performative. Nothing ever felt safe.

Every conversation became a battle of wills. Every family gathering left Samira emotionally exhausted. The pain wasn't just in the past; it followed her into the present. Into her friendships. Into her workplace. Into the way she second-guessed herself.

Forgiveness felt like betrayal.

How do you forgive someone who was never really there? How do you release someone who never said sorry?

But Samira was tired. Tired of feeling reactive. Tired of being triggered. Tired of holding the story that never gave her peace.

We didn't rush.

Week by week, she allowed herself to grieve the relationship she wished she'd had. She wrote letters she never sent. She cried without judgment.

She practiced saying:

"This happened. I didn't deserve it. But I won't let it define my future."

Bit by bit, she began to feel lighter. Not "forgiven and free," but in progress.

It's not fast work.

But it's the kind of work that lets you breathe again.

Samira hasn't reconnected. She hasn't forgotten. She's not pretending.

But she's not holding it the same way anymore. She's reclaiming her story, one forgiving breath at a time.

Pause here for a moment. Can you relate to Samira's story? It may not involve your parent; it may involve a sibling, a friend, a colleague, a child, maybe yourself. We are not going for speed. We are going for progress.

The Energetic Release: A Ritual Of Letting Go

The Release Letter

This exercise can be extremely liberating and powerful. Like the other exercises, please try to have a support person available to debrief if needed. This work can be heavy yet freeing.

Write a letter beginning with:

"This is what your actions taught me about myself."

Tell the truth about:

- What happened

- What it cost you

- What it changed in you

Then write:

"This is what I'm choosing to release."

Name the emotions, the expectations, the pain.

Close the letter with:

"I release you. I reclaim me."

You do NOT send the letter. You destroy it as a symbol of release.

Fire

Tear

Shred

Bury

Float

Burn sage

Use ceremony

Use prayer

Use intention

Whatever feels sacred and true to you.

Reflection Exercise: Are You Ready to Release?

Sit with these questions:

1. What expectation am I still holding onto? (An apology? Understanding? Validation?)

2. What part of the wound is still hurting? (Be specific.)

3. What do I gain by holding on? (Be honest.)

4. What do I lose by holding on?

5. What would peace feel like in my body? (Visualize and feel it.)

6. What version of me is waiting on the other side of forgiveness?

Your healing knows the timeline. Your heart knows the way.

I release what no longer belongs to me.

I choose peace over resentment.

I honor my pain and my healing.

Forgiveness frees my future.

I reclaim my power with compassion.

My peace matters more than my anger.

I am allowed to move forward, even without closure.

I trust myself to heal at my own pace

"Forgiveness is not about changing the past. It is about refusing to let the past change you into someone you do not want to be."

Closing: This Is Liberation

You are moving from pain to peace, from holding to healing, from surviving to sovereignty, from carrying the wound to the wisdom that comes from releasing it, from waiting for freedom to choosing it.

That kind of movement is not linear. And it is not easy.

Forgiveness is one of the hardest practices we ask of ourselves: not because we are unwilling, but because forgiveness directly touches our emotions, our memories, and our sense of safety. In many ways, unforgiveness is the mind's attempt to protect us. It says: if I stay guarded, if I remember the hurt, if I don't soften, I won't be hurt like that again.

That instinct makes sense. It's survival.

But here's the truth most of us learn the hard way: holding on doesn't actually keep us safe.

What it does instead is keep the wound active. It keeps the nervous system alert. It quietly drains our energy, our peace, and our capacity to move forward.

The longer we carry unprocessed hurt, the more it begins to shape how we see ourselves, how we trust, and how we live. Not because we are weak, but because pain, when held too long, asks for attention.

That's why forgiveness is not about excusing harm. It's not about forgetting. And it's not about reconciling when it isn't safe or appropriate.

Forgiveness is one of the deepest acts of self-love you will ever practice.

Not for them.

For you.

For your nervous system.

For your emotional freedom.

For the woman you are becoming.

If forgiveness has felt slow, complicated, or incomplete for you, be gentle with yourself. You are not behind. You are not failing. You are learning how to loosen something that once kept you alive.

That takes time.

That takes patience.

That takes compassion.

And you are doing it.

With your heart clearer and your mind more grounded, you are now ready for Chapter 17, where we turn this liberation outward and begin to understand how old wounds and protective patterns show up across the landscape of your life.

This is not weakness.
This is wisdom.

CHAPTER SEVENTEEN

The Six Areas of Life

Where Your Critic Lives

"Your inner critic doesn't show up everywhere. It shows up where you're most tender."

You don't experience your inner critic in one general way.

She shifts.

She changes tones.

She adapts.

She hides in different corners of your life depending on what feels vulnerable.

Your critic is not random. She is strategic.

And when you learn where she hides, you also learn where your deepest growth is calling.

In this chapter, we explore the Six Areas of Life, a framework that reveals exactly where your patterns, fears, wounds, and potential are living.

These six areas are universal. Every breakthrough you've ever had, every setback, every pattern, every moment of healing belongs in one or more of these categories.

Let's map them out.

The Six Areas Of Life

The six areas are:

1. Self

2. Relationships

3. Work & Purpose

4. Health & Body

5. Money & Security

6. Joy & Fulfillment

Your critic speaks differently in each one. Let's go through them one by one.

1. Self

The Core of Everything

"The way you speak to yourself becomes the way you live with yourself."

This is the foundation of your life.

Here, the critic attacks your:

self-worth

self-confidence

self-talk

identity choices

intuition

emotional expression

boundaries

dreams

This is where she whispers things like:

"Who do you think you are?"

"You're too much."

"You're not enough."

"You're behind."

"Other people have it figured out."

"Don't make a fool of yourself."

When the critic is loud in this area, you feel:

insecure, unsure, stuck, invisible to yourself

detached from your desires

disconnected from your intuition

This is the area where healing begins, because every other area reflects how you see yourself.

2. Relationships

Love, Connection, & Attachment

"Your relationships expose your unhealed places and your unexpressed needs."

This area holds: family, friends, romantic partners, children, colleagues, and community.

Here, your critic is shaped by:

attachment wounds

people-pleasing

abandonment fears

rejection trauma

learned survival strategies

racialized or gendered experiences

generational patterns

The critic uses phrases like:

"Don't upset them."

"You're too sensitive."

"You should be grateful."

"You have to earn love."

"They'll leave if you say that."

"It's your job to fix it."

When your critic controls this area, you experience:

resentment, overgiving, shrinking, emotional exhaustion

lack of reciprocity

fear of boundaries

guilt for having needs

Healthy relationships require healthy self-worth, so this area closely mirrors Area 1.

3. Work & Purpose

Performance, Identity, and Pressure

"Your critic is loudest where you feel responsible for proving yourself."

This area includes: your career, leadership, creativity, calling and purpose, education, ambitions, and entrepreneurship.

Here, the critic thrives on:

perfectionism

comparison

imposter syndrome

cultural, gendered, and racialized expectations

fear of failure

fear of visibility

She says things like:

"You need to be perfect."

"You're not qualified."

"You're going to embarrass yourself."

"They'll realize you're not that good."

"Don't take up too much space."

When your critic is loud here, you feel: anxious, overwhelmed, avoidant, hesitant, pressured, stuck in preparation mode, disconnected from your gifts.

This area transforms dramatically when you begin trusting your voice.

4. Health & Body

Worthiness, Shame, and Survival

"Your body keeps score and your critic reads the scorecard."

This is one of the most emotionally charged areas.

It includes: physical health, mental health, sleep, nutrition, and movement; trauma stored in the body; body image; sexual identity and intimacy.

The critic uses: shame, comparison, guilt, fear, unrealistic standards, cultural biases, and old coping mechanisms.

She says:

"You should look different."

"You should be stronger."

"Why can't you be consistent?"

"Everyone else is doing better."

"Your body is a problem."

When the critic is active here, you may:

push your body too hard

ignore your body's signals

emotionally numb

disconnect from your needs

avoid rest

internalize shame around getting help

Healing this area requires compassion, not discipline.

5. Money & Security

Scarcity, Stability, and Safety

"Your critic speaks the loudest where your nervous system remembers scarcity."

This area is one of the most primal.

It includes: finances, savings, spending habits, security, stability, opportunity; scarcity or abundance mindset; generational beliefs; racial or cultural narratives about money.

Your critic says:

"You'll lose it."

"You're irresponsible."

"You don't deserve ease."

"You're going to mess this up."

"There's never enough."

"You can't trust yourself with money."

Money triggers survival instincts.

And survival instincts trigger old programming.

When the critic runs this area, you feel:

fear

guilt

shame

chronic stress

impulsive or avoidant

stuck in "just enough" mode

This area often transforms when you change your beliefs about worthiness, not numbers.

6. Joy & Fulfillment

Pleasure, Desire, and Permission

"Your critic fears your joy because joy is expansion."

This is the area people overlook, but it is essential to a full, aligned life.

It includes: hobbies, rest, play, creativity, travel, spirituality, pleasure, desire, fun, exploration, and connection to self.

Here, the critic says:

"You don't have time for that."

"You need to earn rest."

"You haven't done enough yet."

"Be serious."

"Stop being selfish."

"Other people need you."

When the critic suppresses this area, you experience: burnout, resentment, emptiness, lack of excitement, numbness, feeling like life is only a responsibility.

Joy is medicine.

Fulfillment is fuel.

Pleasure is information.

Desire is direction.

Your critic wants to limit joy because joy expands your sense of possibility.

Which area, or areas, can you identify that need some intentional attention? Let's explore.

Your Critic Has A Home Base: Where Is Yours?

Everyone has one area where the critic lives the loudest. For some, it's relationships, body image, work, money, self-worth, visibility, rest, or ambition. It could be one of these things or several.

Think about which area causes you the most:

anxiety, guilt, shame, avoidance, overwhelm, people-pleasing, and/or overthinking

That's your home base.

Once you understand your home base, you understand the root of your patterns.

A Story: The Critic In My Six Areas

There was a time when my critic lived in all six areas, loudly.

But her home base was self-worth.

Because when that area is unstable, the others become unstable too.

My critic told me:

"You need to prove yourself."

"Don't take risks."

"You need to stay small."

"You're not ready."

And she showed up in:

relationships (overgiving)

work (perfectionism)

money (scarcity)

health (ignoring rest)

joy (feeling guilty)

When I strengthened my self-worth, all the other areas shifted.

This is how powerful this framework is. Simple but not easy.

Just remember: something can look or seem impossible until someone does it. You can do anything if you believe you can.

Reflection Exercise: Mapping Your Six Areas

Before you begin this exercise, pause and remember:

Awareness creates choice.

When you map your critic across these six areas, you begin to see not only where she holds power, but also where you are ready to reclaim it. This activity is about more than identifying pain points. It's about identifying growth edges.

Each rating is a doorway into a conversation with yourself. Once you've identified where the critic is loudest, don't stop there. Take a moment to define what you want for that area.

Write down your ideal vision, your goals, and, most importantly, describe how you will feel when you achieve them.

When you link a goal to an emotion, you make it real. You activate your brain's Reticular Activating System (RAS), the internal filter that begins noticing people, opportunities, and choices aligned with what you desire. It's how your mind starts collaborating with your intention.

To avoid overwhelm, plan to do this exercise across the span of a few days or a couple of weeks. This gives your brain the opportunity to really think about your next steps, and to problem-solve while you are resting.

Step 1: Become aware of where you are

Be honest with yourself. Note the facts about each area, not feelings yet. Once you've noted the facts, then note how you feel about the facts of that area.

Step 2: Visualize your future

If you visualized your life six months to a year from now, what would your life look like in each area? How will you feel? What will you hear? What will you see? Try to immerse yourself in that visual.

Step 3: Rate each area for attention needed

Rate each area from 1 to 5 based on whether paying close attention and using intention in that area could change the circumstances in your life for the better.

(1 = Attention NOT needed | 5 = Attention VERY MUCH needed)

Self: ___

Relationships: ___

Work & Purpose: ___

Health & Body: ___

Money & Security: ___

Joy & Fulfillment: ___

Step 4: Rate the volume of your critic

Rate each area from 1 to 5 based on the volume of your critic. What is your critic saying? Once you have noted what it's saying, counter the argument with facts. We are deciphering between fact and fiction here.

(1 = Calm | 5 = Loud)

Self: ___

Relationships: ___

Work & Purpose: ___

Health & Body: ___

Money & Security: ___

Joy & Fulfillment: ____

Step 5: Reflection

Sit with these questions for each area:

Where does my critic scream?

Where does she whisper?

Where is she silent?

What does this reveal about my story?

What do I want for this area?

How will I feel when I achieve that vision?

What is one small step I could take this week?

This is not just emotional inventory. This is emotional alignment. You are learning to lead yourself with clarity and intention.

I tend to do this exercise in January because it feels like a reset for me. I tend to review in September. You are free to do this exercise anytime that feels right for you.

I lead myself with clarity and compassion.

I am strengthening every area of my life, one
choice at a time.

My critic is a voice from my past; I lead from
my present.

Every area of my life is worthy of love, attention, and
alignment.

Closing: The Final Expansion

Now that you can see where your inner critic lives, something important has shifted.

You are no longer guessing. You are no longer throwing spaghetti at the wall and hoping something sticks. You are no longer working blindly or blaming yourself for feeling frustrated, stalled, or unsure.

This exercise has given you judgment-free awareness, and that matters more than it might seem.

Because if you can't clearly see what's asking for attention, growth becomes exhausting. It can feel random, discouraging, and hopeless.

But clarity changes everything.

What you see here is not a verdict. It's information. It's data.

This awareness may show you where you are further along than you realized: where you have already grown, strengthened, and succeeded. It may also show you where you've been stretched thin, where energy dropped, or where patterns quietly pulled you off course.

None of that is failure. It's feedback.

And now, you get to decide what to do with it.

With clarity comes choice.

With choice comes direction.

And with direction, you can finally create an action plan that fits you.

You've spent time here with the most important person in your life: yourself. That matters. Nothing in your world changes without you. Nothing in your world grows without you. When you understand what has held you back and where your energy truly lives, momentum stops being forced and starts becoming natural.

This is where intention turns into movement.

This is where insight becomes embodiment.

This is where momentum becomes lived.

Be proud of yourself. Be hopeful. Let yourself feel encouraged.

You are no longer circling the life you want. You are ready to move toward it thoughtfully, intentionally, and in alignment with who you are becoming.

And this is only the beginning.

CHAPTER EIGHTEEN

Energy, Alignment, and the Happy Life

Living in Your Own Energy

"Alignment is when your life feels like it finally fits."

You've spent the last seventeen chapters doing the work most people avoid their entire lives.

You have faced your critic, met your subconscious, uncovered your patterns, explored your emotions, strengthened your boundaries, built self-trust, rewired your beliefs, stepped through fear, practiced forgiveness, and mapped your life.

You've done inner labor: deep, transformative labor. And because of that, you are ready to live differently.

This chapter is your bridge:

From healing → to alignment

From awareness → to embodiment

From survival → to joy

From self-criticism → to self-connection

From force → to flow

This is where life starts feeling lighter, clearer, and more spacious. This is where you learn how to live in your own energy.

Alignment: The New North Star

Alignment means this:

Your actions match your values.

Your values match your identity.

Your identity matches your truth.

And your truth matches your life.

When you are aligned:

You move with better ease.

Your confidence rises.

Your intuition gets louder.

Your decisions get clearer.

Your life feels like it belongs to you again.

When you're out of alignment:

Everything feels harder.

Your critic gets louder.

Your body tightens.

Your energy drains.

You second-guess yourself.

You feel disconnected.

Alignment is not about perfection. It's about congruence.

Your outside world should reflect your inside world.

And your inside world should reflect who you truly are.

The Four Capacity Systems

To live a happy, emotionally intelligent, aligned life, you must learn to manage four kinds of capacity.

1. Physical Capacity

2. Mental Capacity

3. Emotional Capacity

4. Spiritual Capacity

When these capacities are supported, your life flows. When they're depleted or ignored, your critic takes over.

Let's break them down.

1. Physical Capacity

The Body's Yes and No

"Your body speaks softly at first, then loudly when you ignore it."

Physical capacity is not just about sleep or food. It's about the felt sense of safety in your body.

Your body tells you when:

You're overwhelmed.

You're forcing things.

You're ignoring your limits.

You're abandoning yourself.

You're misaligned.

Signs of physical misalignment:

exhaustion, tension headaches, heaviness, burnout

cravings, emotional eating, shutdown

restlessness

Healing physical capacity requires:

rest without guilt

nourishment without punishment

movement without shame

breathing without rushing

Your body is not the problem.

Your body is the messenger.

2. Mental Capacity

The Thoughts You Feed Yourself

"Your mind is a garden. What grows depends on what you water."

Mental capacity includes: focus, clarity, patterns of thought, inner dialogue, cognitive load, decision-making, and boundaries with information.

Signs of mental misalignment:

overthinking

rumination

indecision

distraction

catastrophizing

mental fog

When your mental capacity is low, your critic becomes your default narrator.

To restore mental energy:

reduce multitasking

create margin

slow down the pace

say no sooner

simplify your environment

choose thoughts on purpose

Mental peace is a discipline.

3. Emotional Capacity

The Heart's Capacity

"Your emotional capacity is sacred. Protect it like your future depends on it, because it does."

Emotional energy is: capacity, resilience, sensitivity, empathy, vulnerability, emotional regulation, and boundaries.

This is where old wounds, social messages, gendered expectations, and trauma live.

Signs of emotional misalignment:

resentment

irritability

guilt

people-pleasing

emotional labor

exhaustion

hopelessness

numbness

To restore emotional energy:

speak your truth

stop over-explaining

honor your boundaries

regulate before responding

let yourself feel

stop performing wellness

Emotional honesty is emotional freedom.

4. Spiritual Capacity

The Soul's Alignment

"Your spirit knows before your mind catches up."

This is not about religion. It's about connection to meaning, purpose, intuition, and your inner voice.

Spiritual energy is: alignment, intuition, joy, purpose, creativity, peace, and expansion.

Signs of spiritual misalignment:

feeling lost

feeling disconnected from joy

lack of motivation

feeling like you're living someone else's life

constant hustle with no fulfillment

ignoring your intuition

To restore spiritual capacity:

reconnect to what lights you up

honor your desires

create space for joy

follow intuitive nudges

reflect, pray, meditate, journal, whatever grounds you

let yourself dream again

Your spirit is your compass.

The Happy Life Comes From Three Things Working Together

A happy, aligned life is built at the intersection of capacity, alignment, and intention.

Happiness is not a mood. It is a practice.

It's not an outcome. It is a way of being.

1. Capacity:

Your physical, mental, emotional, and spiritual capacities are supported, respected, and replenished.

2. Alignment:

Your life reflects your values, your needs, and who you are becoming, not who you were conditioned to be.

3. Intention:

You choose your actions consciously, rather than reacting from fear, habit, or old patterns.

When these three are integrated, happiness stops being something you chase and becomes your baseline.

The Signs Of An Aligned Life

When you are aligned, your life will begin to feel different.

You will notice:

more peace, less urgency

more confidence, fewer apologies

more clarity, fewer internal battles

more ease, less guilt

more self-trust, less proving

more joy, less emotional reactivity

Your relationships shift.

Your decisions shift.

Your body shifts.

Your voice shifts.

Your energy shifts.

Alignment is visible.

A Story: The Year I Stopped Running From Myself

There was a time in my life when everything looked successful from the outside, but inside, I was exhausted.

My physical capacity was strained.

My mental capacity was scattered.

My emotional capacity was leaking everywhere.

My spiritual capacity was silent.

I was misaligned but high-functioning: the most dangerous combination.

At some point, I couldn't ignore it anymore.

I started to notice everything: my choices, my feelings, my reactions, my patterns. I began to analyze how I showed up in every part of my life, not because I was trying to be perfect, but because I desperately wanted to feel different. I wanted a different life, so I had to start doing different things.

And wow, did things open up.

It didn't happen overnight. It wasn't always easy. Sometimes I questioned myself. There were days I wanted to run back to my old patterns just because they were familiar.

But I stayed with it, with the support of accountability partners, counselors, and friends and family.

I kept choosing alignment, again and again.

And slowly, everything deepened.

New friendships entered my life: not surface friendships, but sister-friends who saw me fully.

Career opportunities emerged that I would have never been ready for before.

I met my husband: a relationship grounded in truth, not performance.

My relationship with my children grew deeper and more emotionally rich.

I stopped performing happiness and started living it.

My spiritual life also expanded. The more I connected with God, the more I understood myself. My inner voice got clearer. My fear got quieter. My trust, in life, in timing, in purpose, grew.

Alignment didn't make life perfect.

It made it real.

It made it mine.

Today, I still have hard days. I still make mistakes. But I am aligned, and life is better because of it.

Reflection Exercise: Your Alignment Check-In

Rate each capacity from 1 to 5:

(1 = depleted | 5 = overflowing)

Physical Capacity: ___

Mental Capacity: ___

Emotional Capacity: ___

Spiritual Capacity: ___

Then ask:

Where am I low in capacity?

Where am I forcing instead of flowing?

Where am I performing instead of being?

Where is my critic still leading?

Where is my intuition trying to guide me?

Alignment begins with truth.

I honor my capacity by living in alignment.

I choose ease without guilt.

I am becoming the most aligned version of myself.

My capacity is sacred, and I protect it wisely.

Joy is my natural state.

"A happy life is not found. It is created through alignment, capacity, and intention."

Closing: You Are Ready

This chapter marks a final shift: not because the work is finished, but because you now understand how to live it.

You understand your critic, how it formed, how it shows up, and how it tries to take the lead when you're tired, overwhelmed, or disconnected. You understand your wounds, your emotions, your patterns, and the tools that help you work with them rather than against them. You understand alignment, capacity, and what it actually means to live a life that feels like it fits.

And that matters.

Because happiness is not accidental. It is not haphazard. It is not something we stumble into and hope to maintain.

A happy, aligned life is built through intentional practice.

Managing your inner critic is not a destination you arrive at once and for all. It is a relationship you tend, day after day, choice after choice. When we stop paying attention, when we move through life on autopilot, when we ignore our limits or silence our truth, the critic will always step back in and try to run the show.

Not because you're failing, but because that's what unexamined patterns do.

But now, you have a map.

You know how to check in with yourself. You know how to notice when you're forcing instead of flowing. You know how to recognize when you're performing instead of being. You know how to pause, recalibrate, and choose again.

And when you set a direction: when you clarify your values, honor your capacities, and move with intention, the critic loses its grip. Not completely, not forever, but enough that you stay in the lead.

This is what intentional living looks like.

Not rigid. Not perfect.

But conscious, flexible, and responsive.

You will still have hard days.

You will still feel doubt at times.

You will still need to return to these tools again and again.

That's not a flaw in the process. That is the process.

And now, you are ready for the conclusion: the place where all of this comes together, not as theory, but as a way of living. A way of choosing yourself. A way of meeting life with clarity, self-trust, and direction.

You are not chasing happiness anymore.

You are practicing it.

And that changes everything.

CONCLUSION

The J.A.M. Effect™ in Full

Choosing Your Life, Every Day

"Your life changes when you decide to lead yourself."

You've travelled far. Maybe farther than you've ever gone inside yourself.

You've faced truths you once avoided. You've dismantled stories that were never yours. You've named the inner critic that tried to protect you. You've explored fear, practiced forgiveness, reclaimed your voice, reconnected to your body, honored your capacity, mapped the six areas of your life, and chosen alignment over approval, again and again.

This journey was not light. It was courageous. It was transformational. And it was necessary.

And now, you stand at the doorway of something new: not a new chapter, but a new relationship with yourself.

This is where you begin to live the J.A.M. Effect™.

The J.A.M. Effect™: What It Really Means

The J.A.M. Effect™ is simple and profound:

J = Judgment-Free Awareness

You cannot change what you refuse to see, and you cannot grow what you shame. Notice your patterns, reactions, wounds, and growth edges without punishment or pretending.

A = Aligned Action

Transformation doesn't happen in grand gestures. It happens in small, honest choices: saying no when you mean no, resting when your body whispers, speaking when your spirit nudges, choosing what future-you will thank you for.

M = Momentum Through Self-Mastery

Progress is not speed; it's consistency. Emotional intelligence, nervous-system awareness, boundaries that protect your capacity, and habits that support who you are becoming.

This is how you lead yourself: not perfectly, but intentionally.

What Changes When You Live The J.A.M. Effect™

Everything.

You become calmer, clearer, bolder, more grounded, emotionally aware, compassionate, confident, aligned, and self-trusting. And your life begins to reflect it.

Your relationships shift because you show up differently.

Your boundaries strengthen because you honor your capacity.

Your decisions become easier because you trust your intuition.

Your inner critic quiets because you're no longer led by fear.

Your joy rises because you stop abandoning yourself.

This is the work that changes the woman in the mirror.

This is the work that changes generations.

A Truth You Need To Hear

Not every exercise in this book will land for you. That's not a failure: that's design.

This book offers many different entry points on purpose, because growth is not one-size-fits-all. You get to choose what resonates, return to what works, and release what doesn't without judgment.

What matters is not doing everything. What matters is doing something consciously. And doing it again.

The patterns you've explored here were not mistakes. They were strategies: ways you learned to survive, cope, protect, and belong.

But just like clothes we outgrow as teenagers, some strategies no longer fit the life you are trying to live. Outgrowing them doesn't mean rejecting who you were. It means honoring who you are becoming.

Be gentle when old patterns surface, because they are familiar for a reason. Be firm when you catch yourself lying to yourself to protect your ego. Be compassionate when fear shows up. Be honest when it's time to choose differently.

You've done this before. You can do it again. And every time you face a hard truth or do a hard thing, you send yourself one powerful message:

I can.

That belief, right there, is what changes your life.

Your Life Is Not Random. It Is Chosen.

There will be days when the critic gets loud. When fear resurfaces. When old wounds feel tender. When capacity is low.

That doesn't mean you're going backward. It means you're human.

The difference now is this:

You know how to lead yourself. You have tools. You have language. You have awareness. You have boundaries. You have emotional intelligence. You have alignment. You have you.

And that is enough.

Your Daily Practice: Three Questions

If you ask yourself these three questions each day, you give your life the opportunity to continue unfolding in alignment:

1. How am I really feeling?

Judgment-free awareness.

2. What do I truly need right now?

Aligned action.

3. What is one small step I can take toward the life I want?

Momentum.

These questions keep you grounded, intentional, and connected to yourself.

Keep This Book Close

Life is going to keep lifting. That's why this book isn't meant to be finished and shelved. It's meant to be returned to. Keep it somewhere you can reach it. Revisit the exercises. Reread the chapters that meet you where you are.

As one of my mentors, Craig Valentine, says: Don't wait to get ready. Stay ready.

This book helps you stay ready.

Choose Your Life: Every Day

The J.A.M. Effect™ is not a theory. It is a way of being. A way of choosing yourself, your truth, your alignment, your peace, your joy, every single day.

Your life is not waiting on permission. Your life is waiting on you.

And now? Now you are ready.

Go create the life your inner critic once said you couldn't have. Go become the woman your past self prayed for. Go stand in the fullness of who you are.

Because the happiest, most aligned, most powerful version of you is not in the future.

She's here. She's ready. And she's yours.

INTERVIEWS

Source Material for Slay Your Inner Critic

Stacy

Going through…watching parents struggle with addiction, mental health and then cancer. Their life journeys and struggles were a massive life challenge and upbringing. My dad passed in 2012, and my mom before that. This was a lot of my life.

Having a child with special needs. This was somewhat of a surprise.

Having a partner with a chronic illness, Sickle Cell and Depression.

Still working through some of the challenges. Some of the challenges I've had to work through.

I've learned that I can navigate any situation…a belief born of what I've been through. Fear does not play into stopping me. Sometimes it's just one foot in front of the other. Just need to get to tomorrow and do the next task. Just need to go to sleep and get up and keep going, one foot in front of the other. The next day always comes. Other people help as well…support and having people to discuss things are really difficult. If you can speak the truth out loud, it's not as scary, and there's always a solution on the other side.

Sometimes I've chosen poor relationships, not caring about it at some points of my life. Self-sabotage, surrounded myself with people who were not really there for me and being ok with that. Being busy and staying ultra-busy, don't feel and don't think, just do. Spent many years doing that. Even now have a hard time slowing down. Now it's more a personality thing as much as it is coping strategy.

I am absolutely a resilient person.

Resilience is finding a way through anything. Especially the hardships. Most common misconception is that it's not hard and it's easy. It is hard work and consistent work. It is reinforcing work. Resilience is self-talk. Misconception is that you are either a resilient person or not. It can begin at any age. Don't think there is a beginning. Resilience can be quiet but doesn't go away. Need to reach in and pull it out. It can be learned, and it can be taught. Once you have it you have it.

Was speaking at a conference for moms parenting children with special needs about how to get through challenging things and get through other times. Great grandma took me in at age 5; she was 73 years. She always said you can do anything and be anything. Believed her. She was an extraordinary woman. When went through challenging times understood that this is what she was talking about. Always felt she wore a red cape and when she died I had to take on the responsibility of wearing that red cape. When I had a daughter with special needs, I had to ask myself, where was the red cape? Not sure if I had it anymore. Resilience is pulling out the red cape. What is it made of? What is the fabric? If I can visualize my red cape, it helps me get through as opposed to focusing on the negative things going on in my life.

Don't have the energy. It's too hard. I can't do this…these are the messages I hear from inner critic. I'm just done. It's too much. Being overwhelmed.

Fact-checking: is that true? Is that true what you're saying? Often times it's not. Have had anxiety all life so a counselor advised me to fact-check. Going to support people and talking to them and fact-checking. Sometimes they can see things objectively.

Belief in the bigger picture, the intellectual part of me helps me to get through the hard times. What is my goal? What do I want to do? It's bigger than this moment in time. Otherwise get stuck in the now of what is happening. I can do anything, no matter what problem comes there has never been a time I couldn't get through something. Keeping the bigger picture in my mind during the hard times.

My friends are part of my support system. They are the people that I believe when they tell me things. I trust them. Sometimes I don't like what they are saying but ultimately it gives me pause and I listen. Don't have a lot of family but very good friends help me through.

I'm a work in progress when it comes to saying no. Struggle to get everything done. Push self a lot. If it's not me, it won't get done, sometimes struggle with this thought. It's a practice thing. Not comfortable always. But have to develop boundaries or family is negatively impacted. So learned that even when I'm uncomfortable, I know I have to do it.

Hard to say no because I believe when opportunity knocks you have to take it. Sometimes saying no feels like a missed opportunity. Don't want to say no to someone or be rude to people I like who may be asking. Worry about what the person may say, don't have the emotional energy to deal with the person's reaction.

Difficult to put own needs first. One of my biggest challenges because my family has needs from me. Have to find compromise, I can help until this time and then I need to spend some time to self. Finding a balance where I'm giving and also finding time for myself. Sometimes people will try to push the boundaries. It's a challenge.

Advice: It will be ok. I would reinforce to go for my dreams and always have a plan B because things don't always work. It's ok if things don't always work out. Believe your own story and voice. Looking back, I wouldn't take on other people's truth over my own.

Candace

Low self-esteem. Going through a trauma doesn't help self-esteem. Still working through it. Surround myself with people who don't make me feel I have to change and that I'm enough.

Opinions of others and not thinking of the opinions of others weighs on my mind. Hard to not let other's opinions stop me from doing things. Still working through it. Remember why I'm doing something and stay true to that. Pay attention to who I hang around with.

Stigma, when going through things with mental health there is a stigma. Took a long time to come to the conclusion that I don't have to explain myself to people. Be worthy of my explanation. People question process and I need to be ok with my process.

Practice not caring about the opinions of others and distinguishing whose opinion matters and whose opinion doesn't. After going through a trauma I was immediately bombarded with having to explain the actions of others and the actions of myself for a good 3 years. Tried to explain why I was doing what I was doing and it was getting exhausting. I thought, they aren't going to do anything with this information so why am I giving it out? It can be frustrating.

Not my circus, not my monkey.

Consider myself a resilient person. Resilience to a lot of people is going back to the way you were. You might never end back the way you were and this does not mean you are not resilient. You're still resilient, you're just new. Was always trying to get back to the original person that I was but that was never going to work because I was not that same person anymore. It hinders us to have the expectation that you can be the same person you were before the experience you may have gone through.

Inner critic messages: imposter syndrome when experience tiniest bit of success. People don't actually like you. You're embarrassing yourself. Changing careers…worried about what people would think. You're going to fail at this and what are people going to say about you. To combat that, look up statistics. Look up the facts. Then can see what track I'm actually on, it helps me combat the inner saboteur. Doing the best I can with what I'm given.

Having a person that I can "this is what I'm feeling and I need you to be honest with me", unpack thoughts. Having that objective voice helps. After a while this helps me to be able to have the conversation by myself, still working on this. We have to show more compassion to ourselves.

To get through challenging times, I try to practice empathy for myself without feeling I need to shame myself. Boyfriend has been an amazing support and he's taught me a lot about practicing mindfulness. Started to take time if I need it and not worry about what people think if I need to take time. Very empathetic with others and learning to be empathetic with self.

Have a friend who is an amazing support. She has been my friend since we were 3 years old. Seen each other through the weirdest and best of times. Her parents are also amazing supports for me. My mom is always a great support even if she doesn't always understand what I'm going through. My dad's side of the family have always been a huge support. They were quick to surround themselves around me when I went through my trauma. It was nice to have them validate me.

Trauma: in May of 2016 my fiancé died by suicide. I was 20 years old. It was eye opening and it was absolutely terrible. In the end it was beautiful because found self through it.

Not good at saying no to people. Still practicing this. I know I'm a people pleaser. Don't like confrontation and have a fear of displeasing people. I would rather just say yes as opposed to disappoint someone. This is a work in progress. Whatever I think in my head is usually the most extreme. Start thinking about is this going to hurt me more than it will be to please them.

Depending on the person will determine comfort level in saying no. If the positive outweighs the positive, then likely will say yes. After fiancé's death said yes all the time, it was very detrimental to mental health. Now that practice saying no and seeing how people will react, it gets easier.

Be patient with others and don't put too much pressure on yourself. Had an intense desire to please when younger. Focus more on self and mental health so that you are more mentally capable when the challenging times come. Put yourself first.

Daria

Failed marriage.

Being abused.

Not seeing children for years.

Underlying thing that I have is hope. Not seeing kids and failed marriage, hope kept me going and kept me alive. Always had hope that there was better and that there was more. This was not the life was meant to live. There was going to be better. Therapy helped, speaking with trusted friends helped. Was very fortunate. Shut self off from the world for a while as was embarrassed about what I was going through.

When opened up it made me vulnerable, thought what would people think of me, they would have done it differently, fear of judgment. Felt good sharing the story because they helped me process my feelings and helped put things in perspective. Sometimes need cheerleaders in your corner.

When think of the hardships I have gone through, yes, I'm a resilient person. I'm like a cat, no matter how you throw me I will land on my feet. I refuse to let anything that has happened to me make me a victim. Refuse to be a victim. My mom has chosen to be a victim and as much as I love her I knew I did not want to be like her.

Resiliency is ability to move forward in the face of despair, no light at the end of the tunnel, in the face of challenges. Continual effort to move forward and not allow what has happened to you hold you back. A misconception of resilience and healing is something that happens to you as opposed to something that you have to actively work at. You have to put the effort into becoming more resilient. It's an action. Something you have to do, not something that just happens to us.

You don't deserve success. You're not supposed to be in front of the class teaching. You don't have the experience. Imposter Syndrome. You're not as good as you think you are.

Keep on carrying on and be myself. The more I get good feedback from employees, school, students, etc. When hear from students especially that I've had an impact on their life, it helps me to keep going. Helps me squash the voice. I have a lot of great info to share with people, gifting them my experience. The positive feedback reinforces that I'm doing the right things. Having faith in self helps. When give in, victim mentality, woe is me. Get out of it real quick as don't like victim mode at all. To get out of victim mode, call it for what it is. So you're feeling sorry for yourself right now, let it soak in. Let's just sulk for a minute, but we're not staying there.

Give it the attention it needs but only for a short period of time. "I see you" is what I say to it.

Survivor instincts, fear of failure, always wanting to improve self, never giving up.

Having faith. Understanding life's purpose and recognizing that I was put on this Earth to help make positive impact in people's lives. These things keep me going.

Support system: husband, daughter, dad to a certain degree, and closest friends. Was seeing a therapist in the past.

Boundaries is something that I've been more focusing on in the last 6 months. Been practicing it more with mom and daughter. They are two of the most challenging relationships that I have.

Mom uses guilt when she wants something from me. She uses manipulation. She will say things like "You don't call me. You will miss me when I'm dead." Don't have a good relationship with mom. Not a person I would choose to hang out with. Want to but it's a toxic relationship. Three years ago put a boundary up because took her out for mother's day and she brought up the abuse that dad inflicted on her. Stopped her and told mom that I can't be the person she talks to about this. I have to heal from my trauma. Mom didn't like that and told me that she doesn't have family here and that I was all she had, but I told her I couldn't listen to her talk about the abuse my dad inflicted on her. She got really mad. Relationship has really taken a turn for the worse since then. Will probably regret it one day when she's gone but not prepared to do anything different at this point.

With daughter, she's very deep and she can be a lot. Have to be in the right headspace to really take it in. Sometimes don't see eye to eye and I'd go into her room and try to make peace and try to mend and the last couple of times I just stop. She can be up and down with her emotions. Can take me down a rabbit hole real quick. I have had to develop healthy boundaries instead of riding the wave with her.

Makes me feel guilty to have to put up these boundaries. But have to preserve self.

Struggle with practicing the healthy boundaries. Don't know if knew what healthy boundaries were. The more I find that people drain me, that's when learned to put healthy boundaries up. Have a friend that I've had to distance myself from because for the last 3 years it's the same things over and over again. No matter what we talk about, there is no forward movement. Want to surround self with people who want to move past things and don't want to be in victim mode.

Honor your truth. If I listened to my truth, I may not have been in the relationship I was in or I may have left the relationship sooner. Being in that relationship was not operating in the best version of self. Who are you and who do you want to be? Shell of a person for a while. Had I known more coping strategies and honoring my own integrity.

Bob

First challenge was at birth. It is my cornerstone that gets me through hardships. Had an aided birth. Mother was going to die with the pregnancy. Father had signed papers to terminate. Nurse came in and found me on the bed. Mom didn't realize I was born. Mom was out of it. Survived birth. Pretty spiritual person. Believe I have a purpose here on Earth.

Being an immigrant that migrated here at 8 years. Stayed until 11 years old. Challenge was trying to adapt to Canadian Society. Me and my brother were the only two colored boys in school. Learning to adapt to a primarily Caucasian Society was a great challenge. Was from the Caribbean. Area born and grew up was in the heart of a sugar cane plantation. Spent a lot of boyhood days in the fields. Behind the factory there was a big white mansion. Slave masters headquarters. Village was a Hindu village with surrounding areas with African people. There was always a stigma about the mansion on the hill. Heard the stories from parents, when dad was a boy the white people would try to run you off the road. Racism was strong. Coming to Canada and knowing racism exists, was afraid of coming to Canada due to being afraid of white people.

Did not get landing status when came to Canada. Canadian government told them to leave. Dad had some contacts. Went back to Trinidad. Those 3 years were hard because big question mark over our future. We had sold everything so basically fresh start in 3rd world country. It was difficult. Parents had to go to Mexico and file from there. Didn't know if would make it. On my birthday, my dad opened the mail and they were granted residency in Canada. When came to Canada had to start over again as didn't have anything.

New beginnings.

Faith brought me through the different hardships.

Yes, very resilient person because never gave up hope that things would get better. Sometimes progress is slow and sometimes it's non-existent and so have to keep faith and believe things will get better. Living a success story now. Have own home, beautiful family, good job, good career. I'm a success story.

Resilience is the will to continue jumping the hurdles of life. Everything hangs on spirituality and the existence of a higher power.

Inner critic is like the devil. You're not going to make it, not good enough, you're bound to fail. Grew up with racist remarks which contributes to the inner critic messages.

My cornerstone is knowing I have a purpose on Earth. Positive self-talk is what I use to move through challenges.

Faith and spirituality, music, help through the challenging times. Used to fall asleep to music.

Support system is God. Understand root source. Bob Marley's music. Any great intellectual or conscious person would follow.

For a long time always said yes. People frequently talk about 3 strikes but would give people over 10 strikes. We're all human having a human experience. Always give people a chance.

If said no, not sure what would happen. Maybe people would lack faith in me or they'd know I'm pushing back. Many people mistake kindness for weakness. Know not weak, just being the good person I choose to be.

Learning not to give as freely.

Faith in God pulled me together. Had dreams and people talk to me. Humble yourself and you will reach further, uncle said this to me but he did not realize he said it. Received messages from other people. Higher power is trying to make connection with me. My advice: humble self sooner and humble self more than I did. Not sure how it would have changed the outcome of my life. Quite satisfied where I am in life right now. Value the experiences that I had as I wouldn't be the strong person that I am today.

Steve

Relationship with dad, relationship with Canada, being from the Caribbean and then having immigration issues has been a challenge, and then my adventure as an entrepreneur. When I was younger I would rebel more, coping mechanism. Procrastination was an issue, avoiding the situation. Blaming others instead of accepting it myself. Didn't get me closer to where I wanted to be. So I had to hone in on some techniques. Develop patience, communication skills, doing things that built confidence. Became more self-aware. Became more financially responsible, downgraded expenses. Journaling and affirmations were other grand techniques to better manage these, not challenges but less of a problem.

100% yes I am a resilient person. Have been knocked down several times but still here. Have seen others get knocked down a lot harder and they got up so I saw that it was possible. If they could do it then so could I.

Definition of resiliency: a person's ability to positively overcome a situation. Misconception, people think that they are not resilient but we are all resilient in certain ways. As humans we all know struggle.

Common messages change over time. When I was more unstable my inner critic would tell me I'm too short, I'm incapable, different degrading types of things. That's not necessarily today. About 4 to 5 years ago realized that was not healthy and so after journaling and doing affirmations I realized: what have we gotten ourselves into? We've only gotten started. We got this. This is easy work, just take one more step. I do get periods: you're not giving it all you got. Can we actually do this? Why are we doing this? Get a combination of both now. Inner critic is more of a friend than an enemy now.

Giving up is not an option. While alive we have an opportunity to make the most of it. We can always pivot but we cannot stop moving. Stopping is the equivalent to death whether you are still breathing or not. Sometimes need rest in order to build back up to get through things. Have to let the heaviness sit for a while and rest, then go and face it. There are times when feel overwhelmed but know life has ups and downs. Need to go through the highs and lows because that's the flow. Have to accept it and when in the lows accept it for what it is and don't give it too much energy because this too will pass. Can't appreciate the highs if you don't go through the lows. Makes your experience so much better.

My whole self helps me go through the hard times. I'm totally committed. The potential of being able to, tickles me so much, laughable that wasn't so committed before.

Support system: family, journal, and team. Family, it can be an emotional kind of relationship but at the end of the day they are still my family. My journal is critical because it is you speaking to yourself as your own friend as opposed to thoughts in your own head. Like to read it back. Professional team, they help me accomplish the things I want to do.

Used to find it difficult to say no. Used to be a people pleaser. Used to think I was an extrovert but realize I'm an introvert. I was always exhausted and did not have time to better myself. Learned that saying no is incredibly powerful. Can say no now because have more energy. True to self so have more energy to do things. Learned saying no contributes to energy.

Went from one extreme to another. Went from saying yes to everyone to cutting everyone off. Probably not the healthiest way to deal with things but it was easier to say no. Still working on the balance. Sometimes spend too much time on work-related items and say no to people and relationships more than probably should.

Advice to younger self: Start journaling. Never considered myself to be a strong writer. Thought was a science kid. Didn't realize my creativity or who I was and who I wanted to be until I started to journal and read back what I wrote. Think journaling earlier would have helped me be a more effective person in society from a younger age.

Corey

Top 3 challenges and coping mechanisms:

Had a breakup of a 20-year relationship. Childhood sweetheart. Had to let go of the relationship. It was hard. Families were involved.

Give up on childhood friendship. Big life event. Had to put self first as didn't do that in the relationship. Had to face what comes from the breakup and face the unknown. Took a leap of faith that would land ok. Grew up together, so was hard. Lots of confronting fear and unknown. Confronting shame, how could I do that to someone. He had some functional depression. Had to do this for me. Got help to get through it. Knew this was bigger than my family. Family was emotionally invested. My sister was really great. My mother was besties with mother-in-law so couldn't go to her. Went to a counselor. Didn't know how to reach out to friends. An acquaintance of mine went through a breakup and we ended up having lunch together. She recommended a book, Scaredy Squirrel. It helped. Learned could reach out to people. Realized I wasn't completely alone. Journaled a lot. Did crazy journaling.

Had a job, failure to listen to my intuition and not listen to red flags. Was a highly abusive workplace and abusive boss. By making a move away from the job, burned a bridge. Went with a competitor and her feelings were hurt. On the first day of the new job knew made a mistake. Didn't listen to my gut. Made a mistake, move on, didn't do that. Husband was risk averse. Couldn't tell him that wanted to leave 3 days after starting the job. Suffered through it. Wrecked myself in the process. Saw myself diminishing and becoming less of a person. Breaking down. Didn't listen to myself and honoring myself. My inner critic was huge. Kept me there for 6 months. It was enough to cause considerable damage. Think had PTSD after that. Didn't know what an abusive relationship looked like until had a work relationship like that. Wondered what kind of day would have that day anytime saw the person. Had a couple of friends that saw what was happening and validated what was happening. This was very powerful. Confirmed that I was not losing my mind and that I was shrinking. Reached out to husband and confessed what was happening and we figured out how to make a plan. Talked about it with friends and partner, developed a plan. In one day, became 10 feet tall and owned my power and left. Don't know who that person was, but in a meeting said this is enough, this is over. Friend took a photo of me on that day. The smile on my face and the relief I had was extraordinary. I did all the wrong things, insulated myself, embarrassed, didn't listen to self. Dug deep and did what had to do. Did a lot of things wrong but it was good learning. It was awful but I learned so much about myself. Lesson in listening to gut. Had a fear people would think I got fired if I left within the first week. Didn't honor self.

Resilience: I am a resilient person. Misconception: you have to push through and suffer through situations. The most resilient move is to tap out, thanks but not my circus. We have this idea that there is nobility in pushing through and suffered through. The permission to tap out and be ok with it, we don't do it enough. Being authentic to self and learning through the lessons helps to build resilience.

Women have to get it done. It's ok to say no. Too much. Tapping out.

Inner Critic Messages: Had some loud voices. Launched business 7 years ago and remember second-guessing myself and asking self, who are you? How are you going to talk to anyone when you're just learning? Remember pitching a proposal and the HR leader said they were very interested. Put proposal and quote forward and HR leader said sorry, didn't get approval. The rejection made me think: I'm a failure, what are you doing? A loud voice said to me, get on with it. This is ok. This is business. Have to be ok with this. Pick self up. Used the rejection and turned it around and got the business.

Negative self-image stuff, would ask myself where that came from. Recognized the voice and ask where that's coming from. Write things out. When journal or write things down it helps to get clarity. Gratitude helps me see things clearly as well. I do a self-check, helps see things as they are. Honor the sad days. Feeling down, roll with it. Be ok with the ebbs and flows, that's life. Can't enjoy the peak wonderful things if don't honor the down days. When the down days stretch over multiple days, have to reflect and pay attention. Be mindful, may need more than a journal day. May need to spend more time peeling back, may have to speak to someone. Ok with the ebbs and flows and don't panic when have them. Don't rush to feel the happiness to get rid of the sadness. Need to sit in it. Misconception, need to be in a state of bliss every day.

Support system: Husband has been really great at keeping me grounded. He allows me to acknowledge where I am then asks me the questions: why do you feel like that? What are you doing to address that? Can be vulnerable with him. Have a colleague that I speak to about how I actually feel. When have someone to talk to it helps normalize the situation. Sometimes have the feeling: don't belong at this table because people are very smart. Journaling is biggest strategy.

People pleasers: today am much better with boundary setting. That skill has been honed over the years. Have said no and no longer inspired or connected to this cause. Have had those difficult conversations. Not sure if this is fueling my passion. Not sure if it's good use of my time. Remember wanting to belong to community so would say yes, particularly when was single. Sometimes want to belong to something bigger than self but then when in it, what you thought it would look like does not pan out. Was a people pleaser at one time. Went to grad school because didn't want to disappoint my professor. My favorite professor saw potential in me and encouraged me to go to grad school. Thought "Oh, you like me? I could be part of this club?" and so applied to grad school. Mom was happy that I finished grad school. The journey to no longer being a people pleaser:

had to practice saying no. Taking baby steps. Friends were ok. It can be alluring that people want you to be a part of their group.

Advice to younger self: Would tell my 16-year-old self, you can't control everything around you. Be curious. Be open. Be flexible. When you are thrown down a pathway that makes you think, how did I get here, just go with it and you will figure it out, maybe. Not sure if I would have listened.

D.J.

Openly out gay man. One of my biggest challenges was coming out. Have to continuously do it. At 19 came out to family and friends. To overcome, had to sit with emotions and how I was feeling about everything. Was hoping for a simple answer and solution. Talking out loud to self, main strategy. Once it's out there it's no longer in my brain anymore. It's been said, it's real. That lowered the burden and the weight on my shoulders. Took some negative coping strategies, smoked weed. Self-medication to deal with the anxiety. What is this person going to say if I come out to them? Will my best friend still like me? Was doing this to alleviate issues immediately and not deal with the issues.

Completing undergrad was a challenge. Chose to work during undergrad. Not smart enough. Not good enough. Shouldn't be here. Better communicators and better students in the class. Try to rationalize instead of catastrophize. Realized I was overthinking. Shared with others. Have a great support system in my life. Talking out loud to best friend or partner, then someone else can know you're going through something. Sharing the challenge and being vulnerable. Not always having to put on a brave face.

In 2nd year University one of my best friends passed away very unexpectedly and tragically. It was really putting my healing in the hands of others. Difficult to cope with everything all at once. Talking through all of that with others. Self-medicating was in there too. Took time to celebrate the small successes. Taking the time to understand this is progress.

Yes, I am a resilient person. Resiliency and strength are synonymous. Misconception, when someone is perceived to be resilient the thought is they can handle everything.

Taught to internalize a lot of pain and suffering. Was a national gymnast. Brought a lot of this going forward. Holding your own. May be thrown challenges but will always overcome. Misconception: oh you're strong you will handle it. People not putting in the time to really find out if you're ok.

Inner critic: imposter syndrome. Not good enough. Not meant to be here. Someone could do way better. I can't add anything to something that I'm doing. People will think you're stupid.

If choose to listen to the voice, there is a little bit of complacency. If give in, then give it the power. Stepping out of the comfort zone, getting comfortable with the unknown. Gain new experiences and skills, this can be exciting and can give fuel.

Can get shy and anxious with new things. But see it as an opportunity to learn new things. Push self to be uncomfortable especially when you know you are capable of doing it.

Know I need to show up for myself and be kind to myself in order to do the best for me. Self-care, workout, cook, read. These are things that bring me joy so that I can be there for myself and be that support that I need for myself. Hopeful and optimistic, sticking to those traits, use that to be there for myself. Support system: have a fantastic support system. Live with partner. Unload, rant and tell him about my day. Talk through everything. He's really good at picking up when I'm tense or frustrated. He keeps me calm and collected. Have a really good relationship with my mom. Talk a lot. Bounce back with each other. Mom comes to me for advice once in a while. Have an open line of communication. I have some true best friends that I can go to about anything. Boss at work, have a fantastic relationship. He is a great mentor and leader. Can go to him about anything. Feel pretty lucky.

Definitely a people pleaser so continually working on this. Grew up shy. Whatever I could do for people was my way of communicating and showing them that I'm a good person. When have to say no then it's like a visceral reaction. Don't want to disappoint.

More difficult to say no in a work sense. Must be pressing if someone is asking me to do something. Is this a priority? Do I have the capacity to be there for someone else right now or am I barely present with self. Understand that my time is equally as important as someone else. Take a step back and think about it.

Believe we can learn from the past so like to live in the present. Not necessarily anything bad that want to change. Going through those experiences molded and shaped me in some way. Would tell self to say yes to things unknown to me. Stop worrying about what other people think. Worried about what other people thought of me when I was younger. Half the time they're not thinking about me anyways so need to stop worrying about what other people think of me.

Taylor

Was working somewhere and was in a situation where I was working my butt off doing so many things and wearing so many hats, and then when positive things would happen, never heard good job, but when negative things happened, I was targeted. It was tiring and exhausting to deal with it. Decided that would not be held as a hostage so started to bring in new staff. When I started to show new faces then people started to realize, they felt threatened. New staff was liking me so old staff had to be nicer. Started to change the structure, strategy that used. Exerted my power. Sometimes when people know you have a certain nature they take advantage of that. Wasn't going to allow them to make me a victim. Showed them who's boss.

Being a single mom with two kids. Didn't anticipate. Was in a relationship with my ex for 15 years. It became very abusive, verbally and emotionally, to the point where I was fearful. Was scared. Decided to take my power back. It was a process. Needed to be more empowered and get stronger. Needed to get certain things because had become so numb. Was afraid, the unknown was scary. Had to do what was best for me and my kids. The toxicity was holding me back and maybe even holding him back. Couldn't take the abuse anymore. Two attempts were made to reconcile as separated before. Finally had the courage, got myself set, started building my career. Gained independence. Built up the strength and the courage and then said he had to go. He was not happy at first. The anger and the outbursts were too much. The more I was silent and focused on self, the more I was able to gain the courage. It wasn't an overnight thing. Understood this would be a process. Have a desire to go out there. There are a number of women who look up to me and who I counsel. I looked at myself one day and looked in the mirror and asked myself what would I advise myself. I wanted to be an authentic person. Didn't want to be that woman that couldn't listen to self but always helped others. Knew God had so much in store for me. Needed to break the chain of the bondage that I was living in. Was trying to help other women while I was living in challenges. Had to rebuild confidence.

Yes, I am resilient. 100%. I have a personality where I keep pushing through. There are moments where I want to give up or think "I can't do this." I was feeling overwhelmed just an hour before this conversation. Had a good cry. Then went about my business and did what I needed to do. Possess qualities that make me resilient.

Misconception about resiliency: you can still have weaknesses and still be a resilient person. You don't always have to be strong to be a resilient person. Sometimes we put too much pressure on ourselves to be strong. Can be going through a healing journey, can be broken and still exude resilience. Understand that you have moments. Don't always have to be strong. Can have a moment of weakness and still be resilient.

Inner critic: What doesn't it tell me? The biggest thing I struggle with is that's not good enough. Wait until this gets better. Just one more thing. Have to fight that. If constantly wait for the right time then it won't come. I understand to trust God's timing but if the spirit is speaking and you feeling it, go for it. God will create the final product.

Have to push myself because if I don't do what I know I should be doing, it will make me feel more discouraged and angry with myself. This puts me further back. Listen to a lot of encouragement. Read and listen to a lot of positive content. Promised myself that I will no longer become enslaved to my thoughts. Have to let go of the attachments and certain outcomes, and can't necessarily focus on the outcome. Looking way too far ahead. Release outcome in mind, go with the flow. Outcome will eventually show itself. Focus on the here and now. Be present and focus on the moment. Can have a vision but can't get hung up on it. Don't let fear get in your way. Trust yourself. Go for it. Release.

Purpose motivates me. What I want to do is done with purpose. Want it to have a meaning. Understand my big why. Do it for my kids. Do outreach. These things feed my soul as opposed to superficial stuff.

Support system: surround myself with like-minded people. Getting more connected with people. Have friends and we go out. Circle of women who encourage you. By nature, we are meant to have a human connection with people. Want to be surrounded by people who will validate me and who I will validate as well. We were created this way. We are emotional human beings. It's how we were created.

Used to be a people pleaser. Had a hard time saying no. Challenges do make you stronger. You learn that you can't give more of yourself than you can. You learn how it turns out. If I don't get a little tingly feeling about it, then not afraid to say no. If I don't feel like doing something, not afraid to say no. Have to protect my space. Only so much my mental capacity can take. Only take on the things that feed my soul. Don't make time for things that don't feed my soul.

Mental capacity: need to be assertive when needed. Need to teach people how to treat you. Many people are not socially aware, don't have social cues or social etiquette. You have to set the tone. How you set the tone is how people are going to treat you.

Advice: Don't want to come from a place of regret. The experiences I've been through are all part of the journey and shape me as a person. Advice: be more confident. But understand why I was not confident at that time, due to trauma. The experiences in my life brought me to where I am. No regrets. My challenges have made me who I am.